Scallywag Books

Copyright © 2016 Scallywag books and Terry Cox

First published in Great Britain in 2016 by Scallywag Books

Email: scallywagbooks@gmail.com

Telephone: 0759732661

Terry Cox has asserted his rights to be identified as the author

of this work under the Copyright, Designs and Patents Act 1988

A CIP catalogue record for this book is available from the British Library

ISBN 978-0-9935547-1-1

Design, Editing and Production by Jose Kerrara, NSLAX, Wework Buildings, Hollywood, Los Angeles, California. United States.

Scallywag Books of London, United Kingdom.

Printed by: Scallywag Books, (complete book packagers) of Hull and London

Printed in the People's Republic of China.

Other books by Terry Cox:

Hessle Road Scallywag 3

Out soon by Terry Cox in 2017

"I was Rod Stewart's double"

Other comedy books published by Scallywag books

Dustbingate

Pizza Wars

The Night Shift

Silent Backlash – now unavailable.

Hessle Road Scallywags

Hessle Road Scallywags 2 – A Brief Encounter in Hull

Other Scallywag books publications:

Mohsen's Rush.

The Highest Emissary

Dustbingate – The Film Script

All Scallywag books are also available on Amazon Kindle.

Out soon in paperback: 2017

by Ian Newton and Terry Cox

Hessle Road Scallywags 4 - The Search for Christmas.

Scallywag Books

Scallywag Books and the above motif are registered trade marks.

and Ian Newton is just a greedy bastard.

All material in this book is the copyright property of Ian

Achmed Newton and Terry Cox and if you copy anything herein.

DEDICATION

This book is Dedicated to all those men, and women, who braved the sea in peace, and war. They risked, and sadly in a lot of cases, gave their lives for the benefit of their country, and to put food on our tables.

Some of the people I sailed with

Stan Becket (R.I.P.)

With whom it was an honour to serve under his command.

Titanic Ted

A seaman extraordinaire, who despite his instinct to try and sink every ship he sailed on, and despite this over whelming urge, somehow managed to keep afloat the ship I was unfortunate to sail on with him.

Albo Cuddy

For his devoted duty in treating everyone as his personal servant, and squeezing his fat arse into a swivel chair. Whilst being a world expert at doing fuck all.

Last, but not least, my old mate, and fellow scallywag. Ian Herbert Newton. Of the 32nd Hessle road Bengali lancers. Whilst I never sailed with him, due to the fact he's sea going career only lasted forty minutes, on the Humber ferry, before jumping ship, and seeking sanctuary in the Grimsby branch of the salvation army.

Acknowledgments

Hull people's museum Whitefriargate Hull. Alison's deli. Hessle road. Hull.

Warning this book contains bad language, sex and mischief.

So, if this sort of thing offends you, sorry but bollocks. The train spotting books are on a shelf in a dimly lit room somewhere (next to the porn). Look out for the mucky Mack mob as on of them will be me.

As you may have guessed I am non-p.c., and don't give a toss about those who are. I will say it as it is, and was, warts and all. So, let's get cracking.

Life is like a motorway it has many turn offs, you just have to pick the right one. Take the wrong one, and you end up at a dead end. You then have two choices, you can stop and except that's where your future lies, or you can get back on life's motorway and carry on till you find your exit (I chose the latter)

I was born in the early fifties, and when you are a kid you think it will last forever, sadly it doesn't. I met my best mate, and now a best- selling author Dodgy Dick Turpin Newton when we were about eight, and we became the Hessle road Scallywags. He has since written Hessle Road Scallywags 2 about his life after leaving school and making his way in the world, and suggested I do the same,

I was unsure until I recently saw someone for the first time in about 20 years, and thought fuck me he's younger than me, and he looked like he had an urgent meeting with the grim reaper. (clearly he took the wrong exit in life). That made my mind up to write this book. Everyone has a life story to tell, but most choose not to, and the only memory of them being on this earth is locked in the minds of their family.

Well, bollocks to that I thought, when I pop my clogs I want people to remember me with fondness, and have a laugh at what I got up to in my life. Not the money I owed them (enough said) and not to have some poor sod wake up one morning in their new house, that the builders had not mentioned was built on an old graveyard, and find out the heavy rain the night before has delivered them a floating coffee table from under the floor boards.

So here we go. I don't know how I got into writing this book but, but like I said I have this mate, who I grew up with and who's name I won't mention as he is not well liked by some of the great and so-called 'good' of the city of Hull. And a mention of his name makes a lot of people in Hull nervous, especially politicians and sphincters start to twitch. My mate has that effect on a lot of people. Can't think why.

How it all started.

Schools out forever

Hull was the biggest fishing port in the world in the 1950s, and sixties. I was born in 1954 on Hessle road. I am one of the original Hessle road scallywags, alongside my best mate, fellow scallywag and best- selling author Mr Ian

Tarquin, Rupert, Achmed, Newton the 74th (because 1974 is probably the last time the greedy bastard bought a pint) Anyway enough of the pleasantries.

This is my story about what happened in life after I left school, and sadly said goodbye to my old mucker to start my adventures of travelling the world at sea, the good, bad, and sometimes sad times. I never lost my sense of humour or mischief making day's as a kid.

So, join me in my mad cap adventures around the world, and at home as we sail into the unknown.

I was fifteen when I left school in June 1969, and within 5 days I was on a trawler, heading for the Icelandic Fishing grounds as a galley boy (welcome to the real world). What an eye opener, I was as sick as a dog for the first five days and as anyone who has experienced it will tell you, it is the worst feeling in the world. Anyway, the rest of the trip was a blur. So, when I got back I decided to take stock. It had been a rude awakening and all the wind ups about first tripper galley boys having beer bottles shoved up their arse, turned out to be old wife's tales thankfully.

When I was thirteen I was lucky enough to take an entrance exam for Trinity House nautical school, which I passed. However, as it was expensive to go, what with the cost of uniforms etc. It was beyond the reach of my parents, so I settled for doing nautical studies at school.

I had good teachers at home as well, in the shape of my Dad and Brother, who were both fishermen as was my uncle (who sadly was washed overboard at sea and was lost). I had an insatiable thirst for learning about ships and the sea. It would stand me in good stead for what was to come. So one day I went down to the board of trade offices in Hull and because I had passed my exams for the merchant navy, I was accepted without having first completed one hundred days' sea time first, which was the rule of thumb. After passing my medical

I was soon assigned to my first merchant ship, which was a B.P. Tanker called the British Maple. In them days you were given a blue seaman's discharge book when joining or leaving your ship, along with a little red seaman's, I.D. book. This was a seaman's passports. I was sorted.

It was bonfire night 1970, and I was going to London, and was to stay the night at the Red Ensign Club before flying out to Abu Dhabi to join the ship. Before I went down to London, the shipping, clerk in Hull said, "Ooh, you will be alright son, you will be back home for Christmas." (Only the the lying bastard didn't say which Christmas.)

Anyway, I checked into the Red Ensign Club, and soon met another young kid, who like me was also flying out to join another tanker. I think he was from a small town in north Yorkshire, but that's beside the point. We hit it off straight away as we were both only sixteen on our first deep sea trip, and also not old enough to drink. That didn't seem to matter to the barman who simply said, "If you are old enough to go to sea son, then you are old enough to have a beer." Well we were happy enough to go along with his wise philosophy, mmm big word, even spelt right. I'm impressed even if I didn't know what it meant at the time. Anyhow me, and my new mate was "chewing the rug", and soon had a yarn bent on. (I will try and tell the story in layman's terms) So if I Digress tough shit, who's telling it anyhow. So bear with me landlubbers and avast there ship mates and all that sea going crap.

As we were talking a mincing voice said, "Hello boys, would you like a drink ducky," Now remember I am only 17 years and from the back water of Hull and totally naïve in London ways or dangers. We turned around and there was this little bloke, dressed up to the nine's in denim. For those who don't know, hear is a bit of fashion history. Seamen had a dress code, fishermen in my opinion where the snappiest dressers of the lot, because they were the only real seamen that went away and came home wearing a suit, shirt and tie as family or friends would meet them in as the trawler landed and they saved the best suit for when they were home on a three-day boozing bender and of course making up time with their lass and because after three weeks away at sea on rolling side winder the old pork truncheon would throbbing. And that's another reason why they saved the best clothes for home.

Now merchant seamen had their own dress code which was denim, and as I was now in the merchant navy and I was happy to conform.

So this odd bloke goes on, "It's alright duckey," he assured us, "I'm in the merchant navy too, and just got back from the states.? Do you want to buy a pair of wrangler jeans? Five quid a pair and there yours?"

Well I only had a tenner to my name, but was fortune was about to smile on me? My new ship mate, let's just call him Tony. I cannot remember his real name, anyhow his parent's must have been coined up and he had plenty of money, because he had about fifty quid in his back arsehole pocket. So, after a bit of bartering we managed to get two pairs for eight quid, which Tony kindly offered to pay for (I was beginning to like this kid).

Well after a couple of more beers it was beginning to take effect on poor old Tony, because he was getting a bit green round the gills and looked somewhat ready to puke, "Need the bog I think mate," he said half gagging, and off he staggered pissed as a newt. After about ten minutes I was getting a bit worried, and also the 'odd' bloke had also disappeared by this time, which I thought curious. So I went to look for him. Rule number one, you always looked out for your mates. Now the bogs in this place where in the basement so off I went in search of my new ship mate.

As I got near I could hear him calling for hooey (throwing up) behind a bog door, and so I pushed the cubicle door open and I was horrified to see the poison dwarf we had met earlier who had flogged us the jeans. He was stood over him trying to take certain sexual liberties and also trying to steal his money. "GET OFF HIM, you dirty bastard," I shouted and he simply turned around and said "It's ok Duckey, I'm only seeing if he's alright. Don't get your knicekers in a twist luv."

"Like fuck you are," I snarled and tried to pull him away. That turned out to be a big mistake and the next thing I remember is, I was sat on my arse having taken this big right hook in the kisser. This "bloke" might have been little but he was also a right hard bastard. At the same time, I couldn't let him get away with what he was trying to do, so I scrambled my way out to the top of the stairs. And to give you some idea of what a posh place the Red Ensign club was (I don't think), they had two bouncers on the door, no doubt to sort out brawling seamen. I quickly told them what was going on and they bolted down quicker than a horny whore's knickers'. It was soon followed by shouting, banging and crashing. I followed the bouncers into the cellar and and when one of the bouncers shouldered the bog door open the poison dwarf landed a sucker punch on one of the bouncer's mush, and laid him out cold. This little "bloke" was turning out to be a real hard knock, he was like a wild animal. But the other bouncer was a battle-hardened campaigner, and soon had the fucker, in a Japanese knacker lock, his hand gripping this "blokes" balls and then started to swing him around by the knackers before continuing to knock ten bells of shit out of the little bastard. By this time the other bouncer had stopped seeing stars and got up and joined in before they hauled him out the club and gave him a good kicking outside and the last I saw of the poisoned dwarf was by the blue light of an ambulance carting him off into the night with his face looking like like it had been through a mincer and a neck brace on, and cutting somewhat of a pathetic figure and now in hysterical tears himself and pointing at the bouncers from his stretcher screaming like a banshi, "They did this!"

Meanwhile I went back to check on Tony. The poor sod, he was in a right old state and was drunkenly crying his eyes out saying he wanted to go home. I helped him get to his feet, and persuaded him to go to his room and sleep it off. It seemed his career was over before it had started.

 As I came back the local plods where trying to take statements on the night's events, but seemingly no one had seen "anything". And the dwarf was never to be seen again, nor was my new mate Tony for that matter. As I had to get up early it seemed he had bolted off at first light and I never saw him again. I often wonder if he joined his ship. As for me, well I was left with two pairs of new wrangler's jeans. But Tony had the last laugh on the arsehole, be-cause he had not paid for them. What happened to Tony I had some trouble getting my head round. I was just 17 years old and the stuff I had seen that happened to Tony, I had never come across before. But it did put me on my guard against talking to seemingly friendly strangers and I put the experience in my men-tal filing cabinet to be drawn on as and when needed.

That day I flew out to join my ship. As I had never flown before it was a big novelty and the flight seemed to go on forever. When eventually me and the other crew members got there, it was a real eye opener. Unlike today's Abu Dhabi it was just a scattering of buildings in between the desert and the sea. Our hotel was one of the first being built and it wasn't quite finished, but it was ok and after being on trawlers, I had learned to rough it and this seemed the next thing to luxury compared to a small bunk on a rolling side winder trawler. We had a couple of days to wait for the ship to arrive as it was in Iran loading oil.

The first day I decided to go for a walk along the quayside, watching the wooden dhows unloading their cargoes of dead goats that were being humped and dumped on the quay side. That night I got my first taste of goat cutlets, and I must admit it, they were really tasty. Well the ship duly arrived we changed crews and we set sail for oriental mysteries of Japan.

I was amazed at the size of the ship, unlike trawlers it was space age: Swimming pool, gym, my own cabin with a bathroom, a crew bar and a cinema. I soon settled into a routine. We also had two cooks (pan- shakers) as they were called on trawlers and to be fair they were good to me and treat me well. The chief cook was called Bill, but the crew called him Nijinsky, because he looked uglier than a fucking horse. He was also unable to say the letter L. Substituting it with the letter W.

This complicated thing's somewhat as the second cook and baker was also called Bill, but old horse face used to call him biw, much to my amusement and many if the piss taking crew. Biw (sorry Bill) was a little welsh bloke who again was ok. But there was also here was something a bit strange about him I just couldn't put my finger on. But I would find out little Bill's secret sooner rather than later.

 The officers on the ship had two stewards, and the rest of the crew had one also known as a mess-man. The mess-man was an 18-carat gold arsehole, who no one liked. He was about 24 and thought he knew it all; he came from Oxford and was always banging his own drum about the place, much to the annoyance of the deck hands, or able seaman to give them their official title.

Well he decided I would become his target for bullying and every chance he got he would wait while no one was about (fucking coward) and he would say things like. "You're just northern peas-ant, and uneducated riff raff." And really try and rub my nose in it every chance he had. But it was always when we were on our own. Well I decided I would just bide my time and justice comes to all wait, eventually.

What he didn't know was I was from Hessle road, the heart of the deep-sea fishing industry, where no quarter was asked for and none given. On Hessle Road you either stood up for yourself or you sank. Run home to your parents and tell them someone was picking on you and likely you would get clout and told, "Well just hit them back and if you can't hit them back kick them back." Whilst I was not a Hessle Road top dog, I could look after myself. And you only took shit for so long.

One day I came out of my cabin heading for the galley, when Mr Gobshite blocked my path, and started doing a Mr Rambo job,

"Morning peasant," he said right into my face and then proceeded to quickly get me in a head lock. That was me done, I had enough and it was show time. I clenched my fist and hit him as hard as I could, right in the knackers. He squealed like a stuffed pig and let go quick as flash and went down clutching his knackers. Moving as fast as I could so he had no chance to get is bearings, I pushed his ugly mug as hard as I could into the hard iron bulkhead bulk-head and as his head met the bulkhead at great speed there metallic 'Dull thud" and his eyes rolled in their sockets and he went down like a sack of horse shit thrown off a coal lorry. The next thing I knew out of nowhere came a big hand that grabbed him by the scruff of the neck lifted him up then pinned him to the bulkhead; it was one of the deck crew.

"I heard and saw what happened you bag of shit," he said growling, "and if you ever touch him again or even look at him the wrong way you will be going for a swim, and it won't be in the pool. Now fuck off and, stay clear or else. He asked me if I was ok and said well-done you saved me a job. "Don't worry he won't bother you again."

From that time on he never tried it again or called me names, but he did end up having a squeaky voice. A couple of days later I was in my cabin reading, when I heard squealing, and giggling in the next cabin, which was little Bill's cabin. And it suddenly dawned on me that "Biw" had caught galloping pyaca, or some unmentionable disease down below, and the mess man was giving him a good reaming out (dirty bastard). But I was wise enough to know to keep my mouth shut and listen and learn as the saying goes, so

I kept stum about it, and another valuable little ditty was placed in the old mental filing cabinet as, "Evidence that may be used against you." If you get my drift. Yes, I was learning fast.

Well we duly arrived in Japan with our cargo and I was amazed, and indeed felt very lucky that I was seeing the world and getting paid for it. We all managed to get some shore leave before heading back to the gulf for another cargo. I was mesmerized by the sheer number of people there, and it seemed no matter which way you walked everyone seemed to be coming the other way. I felt I was indeed fortunate, and lucky to be there. Time seemed to go so quick, and before I knew it we had discharged out cargo of oil and were back in the gulf.

And so we loaded up again this time in Iraq and set sail again for New Zealand. On the way, we stopped at Singapore to take on stores, mail, and new films.

It was xmas eve when we got there. I was stood on the poop deck as we approached the anchorage, and to my horror I saw a pair of hands appear on the handrail, followed by a little grinning Chinese face, then another and another. One of the deck hands explained they call them bum boats, they set up shop on ships at anchor and flog everything and anything. Sure, enough in no time at all the whole stern was covered in all sorts of wares and tears. Later when I had bought a couple of exotic looking things to take home and I made haste to my cabin with my ill gotten gains, and was I in for the shock of my life. A very pleasant shock though. I got to my cabin, and opened the door, I was confronted by a gorgeous Chinese woman in her late twenties with this big cheeky smile.

"It's ok Johnnie," she squeaked in this little cute voice. And she just stood there wearing this gold silk Minnie skirt with the most amazing legs rising up up into a pair of nut cracker thunder thighs. At 17 years I was no different to any any teenager and full of hormones and the old pork truncheon was rising fast. "I give you good time Johnny." I swallowed a hard lump in my throat with a big gulp, and without no more of a do she was on me like snogging my gob off and giving me a real "tongue-down-the-throat-toe-curling tonsil-tickling- groin-gripper". And the next she pushed me onto the bed pulling down her brief little knickers and we went at like two little bucking rabbits on a spring morning. And fuck my old boots she did things I didn't know were even possible at 17 years old. It was, "Oh, sheer bliss!!!!" for the whole night. And the next morning I work up as she was slipping back into her knickers and I could not take my eyes off this amazing slender body and she had this really erotic way of getting dressed like a reverse strip tease artist, just sliding into her clothes item by item staring urgently into my eyes like she was teasing me. And before leaving gave me this big long wet kiss as I lay in the bed. "You enjoy Johnny?" she asked with a cheeky smile?" And I sighed out aloud. And she leaned into my ear with a shivering hot breath. "You remember me Johnny." and she gave me a card with a number on. "You call I come Johnny." And before leaving put her hand under the bed clothes and gave my manhood a last couple of expert squeezes. "Remember me Johnny," she said and she was gone.

Where the hell had she come from I thought and she had asked for no money. I soon found out when I came out the cabin and half the deck crew were standing outside and they all cheered. It turned out that the deck crew had had a whip round for me and gave her to me as a Christmas present to remember (thanks lads). But alas I would never see my little Chinese nymphomaniac again and would be back at sea soon and back on the hand pump reading mucky books for teenage therapy. We was only anchored for about 15 hours and that was long enough to discharge our cargo of oil and off we sailed again into the sunset. And many night after I stared out into the darkness of cabin and could see the black sky outside and the stars beyond the port hole and wondered where "My Little Chinese Girl." You fall for girls so easy when you are a teenager. But she was exquisitely beautiful. Pity she was a prossi, with God knows how many notches on her bed post.

Well the great day duly arrived, it was Christmas Day, and after finishing my work I went into the crew bar. There was a good atmosphere, booze flowing like water and oiling the friendly banter. It was a real Christmas atmosphere. Shortly afterwards the captain, and his entourage appeared, along with his wife, the chief engineer and his wife. It may come as a surprise to some but yes, wives' of officers are allowed to travel on the ship with their husbands. Anyway the officer big wigs wanted to wish us all a merry xmas and the job was duly done and the entourage moved on. We all tugged our forelocks in deference and the Captain and Chief, along with wives moved onto the galley to bid a "Merry Christmas to one and all,"

The chief cook, as I said earlier was nicknamed Horseface and for some reason had the galley door closed and along with his little kitchen helper had not made an appearance in the crews' bar, but no one gave a fuck because no one liked them. But within seconds of the Captain opening the door, and to coin a phrase often used to describe such scenes, all hell had let loose, with shouting, screaming and all manner of threats being bandied. "What the 'ell's going on in there!" said one of the deck hands. So we all rushed to see what was going on. We heard the captain suddenly shout at the top of his voice, "Don't look ladies!" But it was too late. They had walked in on the cook and caught Horseface in the throes of one of those weird sexual encounters you often hear about happens at sea but rarely see. And Horseface along with another crew member were caught red handed, with Horseface with his trousers down displaying a thumping pulsating hard-on, shiny with olive oil and standing out like a flag pole and about to use it to inspect his ship mate's "port hole" who was bent over a table wearing a black suspender belt, fish net tights and a pair off gussetless black silk women's knickers, that it would transpire later belonged to the Captains wife, and had mysteriously disappeared from the laundry a few weeks earlier along with other purloined intimate female items that had curiously and gradually been disappearing from the laundry. Suspicion was beginning to fall on many who was the "knickers knocker". Well we all knew the culprit now and I couldn't see Horseface worming his way out of this one. Well he was looking to get into a tight spot, but I don't think he had plans on it being this one. We all just stood there is the doorway with mouths gaped open and the Captain and Chief engineer's wives pushed passed in outraged shock with an attack of the vapours, and no doubt wanted her knickers back.

The Captain looked about to explode. "You!, You!" he stammered at the. "Filthy animal!!" The captain screamed, "Your logged! Flogged! and keelhauled!" There nautical terms I should add and he screamed at them, "I want you off my ship in the next port, your sacked!" he said emphatically pointing at them. To every-one's amusement, Little "Biw" looked at him and said, "Well, cap-tain if I am getting sacked I might as well get something out of it." And as casual as you like he just carried on like nothing had and "drove home his point". And the Captain barged passed us, screaming at us. "Sort those dirty bastards out. That's an order!" We all starred at each other in slight disbelief and Horseface was getting stuck in like we weren't even there. We all just shrugged our shoulders and closed the kitchen door leaving then to it and

returned to the crews' bar and carried on with the festivities and got absolutely blathered. And by God did I tie one on.

The days turned into weeks and before I knew it we were back in the gulf loading a homeward bound cargo, but there was to be one final drama, before I would get home. We were soon on our last leg of the trip, stopping of at Cape-town to take on final stores.

We rounded the Cape of Good Hope, and sailed up the Namibian coast. I wasn't feeling to good one morning and the chief steward was called to look at me. I was given an injection and I mean a needle and syringe injection, not any other type. All I remembered then, was the lights went out and I was in the dark land of nod. I later found out that the quick thinking of the chief steward probably saved my life.

After I had suddenly fell unconscious, he threw water over me to shock me out of it. I was later taken to hospital in Walvis Bay Namibia, where I spent two weeks in hospital before being flown home. Apparently, I had some contracted sort of tropical fever, not of the knob pox variety I hasten to add. As if that was not bad enough, agony was piled on top of agony and I had an allergic reaction to the penicillin injection I had on the ship. The fates had been good to me up until then and this was not the end of my first trip I was expecting.

On returning home I had time to reflect on my first epic adventure at sea, and whilst I loved the merchant navy. I still had a niggling urge to go back deep sea fishing to horn my seafaring skills still farther. But I always knew my destiny lay with the merchant navy and I would return because when it came to the sea, the Merchant Navy was my first passion you might say.

I had quite a bit of leave due to me so I had plenty of time to do some soul searching, plenty of soul searching in fact. I caught up on all the local events that had gone on whilst I was away. One day I found myself walking down to the St Andrew's fish docks and found myself on the long since gone wooden jetty and just stare across the water. The wind was in my hair and I could smell the salty Humber in my nostrils and looked out across the dirty brown water and I stared at all the evening blackened silhouettes of ships with their navigation lights on and lined up and moored across the waters just waiting for high tide. I was reminded of my days as a child and how I would come here with a cheap fishing line with my now long gone friends, Isse, Ian and Frankie and I knew my life was moving on. We had all gone our separate ways, and I often wondered were they was. We were inseparable in those days, and did we get into up to some shit. I knew Frankie had gone on trawlers and Isse was a committed Landlubber. As for Ian, he was always the nut case of the group, a crazy half caste kid- he wouldn't mind me calling him half caste. Ian was always boiling over with some mad cap money making scheme.

Now I can't resist telling you absolutely crazy story about how we made a bundle of of money when were kids. One day when they were pulling down Hessle Road we were going through this old derelict shop down Colman Street and we found all these the old decrepit rusting push lawn mowers that weren't worth a fart but Ian had this stupid idea. He kept ringing up Lesley's Old junk and Antique shop that was then down Hessle Road and pretending to be a grown up bloke and asking if they had any old lawn mowers. Ian even got some grown up bloke to go in and ask the bloke in Lesley's if he knew where he could get any old lawn mowers and he was willing to pay a quid a piece in any condition, "Just ring me, if you get any old lawn mowers in I have someone looking a for any lawn mowers he can his hands on. I'll pay thirty bob a piece, any condition" The bloke left the man behind the counter with his telephone number. By the time Ian had finished with Lesleys Antique and junk shop the bloke in there must have thought there was a massive demand for old lawn mowers. A week later after some more telephone calls keeping the bloke in Lesley's Antique shop on the boil, and me and Ian loaded up all these tatty old lawn mowers on a pram and carted them off down Hessle Road and where did we end up, but Lesley's Antique Shop and we went in. We must have been about 10 years old.

"Hey mister," Ian said, "you don't want to buy any old lawn mowers do you?"

The bloke in in Lesley's Antique shop snapped our hand off and bought all ten lawn mowers for ten bob a piece. And once outside we bolted as the bloke was on the phone like a shot, no doubt to sell his lawn mowers to his phantom buyer. I often wondered if he ever got rid of those lawn mowers. And that was just one of many of the tricks we got up as kids to make a few bob. And that was Ian, dodgy to the last. Last I heard of him he had disappeared down south. Knowing Ian, he could be anywhere and no doubt ducking and diving somewhere and always loved the girls, as we all did. God where did those days go. Many times in between trips I would find my way to this place and just take in my past and where it had gone. I would often laugh with a tear glazing in my eye. I thought of my friends often. The last time we were together had been to run on the fish docks after school because we couldn't wait to see Hull's first stern freezer trawler, The Southella. It was a great big brand Yellow monster just sitting in the dock. I took a photograph of Ian and Isse standing in front of it.

I knew then deep inside if I didn't' return to fishing now, I might have regretted what was in due time to become nothing more than a passing moment time that would go into the folk lore and history of Hull. I think many of us in fishing suspected a sell out and that something was afoot. But in the years to come few of us would ever have imagined the monster betrayal coming over the horizon that would relegate Hull from one of the greatest and biggest fishing ports in the world to just a northern socially neglected back water left to fester and wither on the vine. Well that's the political story for you. But I cannot help thinking that if my beloved Hull had been some rich posh southern town, they would not have been so quick to suck the blood out of the city. Enough said I think.

At least I can say I was there in Hull's hey day and part of Hulls proud heritage that would go down in history shrouded in a lot of conspiracy theories, and a great deal of controversy. I look at my city now and it breaks my heart. Oh Yee politicians, what have you done? I pray one-day justice finds you with a vengeance. Some people, myself included would even go as far as to call it treachery, and secret deals done behind closed doors. By a spineless government, bowing to pressure from the American government and of course the glorious politicians sold us out at the drop of hat. Hopefully the truth might one day come forth. The truth as they will out. Well more on that thorny issue I will return to my story.

I made my way back home to tell my mother my plans, and as I expected she was more than a little bit disappointed, as she never wanted me to go to sea on trawlers. After the 1968 trawler disaster when three trawlers went down and 58 men were lost, it was an event that haunted all the mothers of trawler men. I assured her that I would go back in the merchant navy one day.

She reluctantly excepted my decision, and she never relaxed when I was away at sea, until I got back home. The next day I went down the fish dock, and looked for a ship, which didn't take long.

Back on Trawlers

It was now 1971 and I was back fishing, and after a couple of trips I went to nautical school to get my deckhands ticket. After 3 weeks training I passed and did my first trip as deckie learner, and what a wake- up call that was. Working 18 hours on and 6 off, one of my jobs was to go down the fish room, cracking the ice for the fish to be laid on. Armed with an axe you had to chip away in the freezing cold at solid masses of ice, it seemed never ending and was bloody hard graft. But it made a man out of boys.

Then as the fates would have it, in 1972 I found myself right slap bang in the middle of my first Cod war with Iceland in a very dangerous game of cat and mouse with the Icelandic gunboats. We more often than not had them on the run. It was round one and after a while a truce was called and near normality resumed, until 1976 the final showdown!!!

I was on a ship called Newby Wyke and we were fishing off Iceland at the height of the Cod war but because of the bad weather we were not fishing but just trying to stay afloat. It turned it was lucky for us, because there was a loud bang from down the engine room that sent an almighty shudder through the whole ship. She was an old ship she was steam powered and what happened was the boiler blew up and we were left drifting without power in bad weather. Fortunately for us there were other ships nearby that immediately came to our aid. After a lot of hard work in danger-ous weather, with the ship rolling like a roller coaster, we man-aged to secure a tow line to another Hull trawler and was towed into the Icelandic port of Akureyri where we moored up at the end of the quay away from the town. But it wasn't long before the Ice-landic rent a mob turned up giving us loads of verbal abuse. To be fair it wasn't the Icelandic fishermen, as all seamen had respect for each other. It was the usual suspects, the great unwashed, workshy and student types and things started getting a bit tasty, when they started throwing coal at us.

Well we had just been swilled around at sea from arse-holes to breakfast and were in no mood to take any slaver from a bunch of Icelandic chav's. We counter attacked and soon had them on the run, and heading for the hills. Things were bad enough as it was, and with moral at a very low ebb, they soon concluded that it was a very unwise decision to start throwing their weight about. It was a short sharp battle and the skirmish was soon over and it was back to reality, and the job in hand.

Because we had no power, our only source of heat, was from the coal fire in a pot belly stove in the fore castle part of the ship where twelve of us lived. The only way to get washed was to put a couple of big steel shackles into the fire until they got red hot and then fish them out with tongs and then throw them into a couple of buckets of cold water (bloody luxury). I shook my head and thought what the fuck am I doing here, compared to the merchant navy way of life this was bloody stone-age. After a couple of days' emergency repairs, we limped back home to Hull. I stuck it out for a couple of more years, and after the Cod- war in 1976 I saw the writing on the wall. it was time to go back in the merchant navy, but before I did.

It was reflection time again and as usual I was drawn back to the wooden jetty close to the lock gates on St. Andrew's. In between trips I was visiting this place more often than was good for me. I suppose it was nostalgia catching up with me. But something else struck me that day. It was 1975 or 1976, I can't recall exactly but things in the industry didn't feel right. I was looking at all the trawlers in dock and for me there were just too many in dock at one time and I had a gut feeling and I knew I was living through the end of days for Hull fishing. And it was then that I made my mind up. I would jump before I was pushed. I think I smelt the wind of change that was coming my beloved Hull and Hessle Road. Times they-were-a-changing as the saying goes and in the years to come those things that I grew up with as child, would slowly start to be taken from me and in many ways I would watch my city and its way of life slowly die. And some of the great men I had sailed with would in later years wither like the figures of ghosts and many would become broken men or destroyed by alcohol and drugs that would become the scourge of many towns and cities across the nation as not just fishing but other industries were ripped out from under them and millions and their children would be callously thrown on the historical shit heap of history. We were no more than industrial cannon fodder to be wasted at the casual indifferent stroke of a politicians' pen over a few glasses of champagne, a cigar, a mutual slap on the back and a big slimy pose for the cameras. Oh yes Mr Ted Heath, I got your number and so did many others.

Out of my own interest I decided to do some research into why it had all gone tits up for our proud fishing industry. Well for those who don't know, get ready for a shock.

There is a place in Iceland (no not the bloody shop) now pay attention this serious stuff now. There is a place in Iceland called Keflavik. It sits on the north western tip of the Reykjanes peninsula. Even now if you do a Goggle earth there is a little mystery that won't show up. So read on.

Now in the height of the cold war it was used by NATO, mainly America as a strategic listening post to spy on the Russians submarines the Americans had a top-secret programme called SOSUS (sound surveillance system). Basically, what it was, was an undersea chain of listening micro-phones, spread out so that when any

Russian sub passed, heading towards America they would be heard and the yanks, would know where they were, nice but there was a problem." The Cod War."

So, what happened next was like a sinister Hollywood film plot. The Icelandic government, told the yanks in no uncertain terms, that if they didn't tell the UK Government to back off, they would stop them using the base and let the Russians use it (not an option) so behind closed doors a deal was struck with our then jelly back Prime Minister Ted Heath to pull out. Ironically the same jelly back toad had a yacht and one day the smug git was out sailing when ooops. The fucker started to sink, and I wonder to this day if he thought, ooh shit now I know how all these thousands of hard working and proud people involved with our once mighty fishing industry feel (I doubt it).

Now for some funny but true stories.

KEEP YOUR HAIR ON

Well with fishing now on its way out I had no choice, I was back big boating as we in Hull call the merchant navy. I had been back in the merchant navy for about a year and was on leave, when I was asked if I wanted to do a run job. Sailing a ship from one port to another delivery time three days with two hundred quid cash straight into my back pocket. A lot of money in those days. I'll have some of that thank you very much I thought. We were to go to Rotterdam, and sail this old rust bucket to Goole and make some easy money. But oh God how wrong I was.

Well all us jolly jack tars duly met at the ferry terminal in Hull. I had never seen such a motley blood thirsty looking crew in all my life and they looked like they had just signed off with Black Beard. And red flags were being raised all over the place here but I couldn't get the thought of easy cash out of my head. But anyway off we went. Luckily my job was simple, I would be the mate for the trip and leave the ship once it was delivered in Goole, the rest would be permanent crew, probably because no fucker else, would employ them except Captain Pugwash. The skipper was a piss head, the engineer looked like he couldn't oil a bike chain, the cook had one eye and by the look of him he must have thought "hygiene" was a greeting "Hello to an elderly female relative". "Hygiene = Hi Jean" - I hate explaining jokes but there are some fucking dim wits out there.

As for the deck crew, I doubt if any of the fuckers could tie their own shoe laces and looked like they had been press-ganged out of that old foreign seaman's knocking shop, The Earl De Grey Pub — not that I would know of such a place in Hull.

The next day we arrived at the ship or a better word might "hulk". It was built just after the war and looked like it had been in one and perhaps two. The skipper called me over and told me the owner was coming down. I didn't expect Aristotle Onasis I can tell you that and I wasn't disappointed. "So, try to look busy," said the Captain with a wink, which I wasn't sure was not a nervous tick. "Look busy!" I thought, I was struggling to look interested. However, a job's a job and so I had a good look around inside and it looked solid and sea worthy, well sort of anyway. So now for the outside I was giving it a good coat of looking at, when "Say Again Sam" came up to me, he was one of the so-called deck crew, I called him "Say Again Sam" because the thick sod was as deaf as a plank and had the I.Q. to match, and would cup his hand to his ear and say, "Say again." I did not have a good feeling about this caper, not a good feeling at all, but focused on three hundred big ones, tax free. And I liked that part, tax free.

"Say Again Sam's" real name was Ron, but hey this is my story!!!!

We were all having a yarn sat on the deck having a cup of tea out of rusting white tin mugs that had long since turned off white and this car sped up to the Quay side with a loud screech and skidded to halt with the help of this lamppost that was knocked clean into the dock. So there this black car foreign in make with steam now pissing out the engine and this bloke gets out wearing a cheap suit and sporting a dodgy very wispy comb over hair cut.

Well "Say it again Sam" took one look turned at me and said, "Who's that tosser?" and, "Who the fuck cut his hair," unlike Mr Diplomacy, I had a notion. The poor sod had a medical Condition, I told 'Sam' to, "Shut up, I think he's the owner and that's a classic case of alopecia," to which the fuck wit Sam cupped his hand to his ear and said simply, "Say again son, Alan who? I don't care what his name is, he wants to find a new barber." I rolled my eyes. "Just never mind Ron. And keep your mouth shut or you'll be swimming home."

After exchanging pleasantries, he went to see the skipper and I thought I would go and see how Mr Manure was doing in the galley. When I went in I waited a while, for the flies, which I assumed were his pets, to settle down on as they swarming around this big pan. He was busy stirring this big rusty old pan of what I presumed was soup of some sort and enquired if he was boiling his underwear. "Cheeky bastard," he answered all indignant, "No it fucking isn't," he replied, with a sort of nervous laugh. "Good pan of soup that is," he said stirring with this dirty big wooden spoon.

"It might be when you take your socks out of it," I said, not being able to stand the smell of rotten road kill any longer. I made my excuses and gave him a big slap on the back. Like what happened next you will not believe. His glass eye shot out straight into the soup with a splosh. "Oh, shit!" he said casually,

"not again." And he starts trying to fish it out with this big wooden spoon, pulling a potato out, then a piece of meat and dipping in and out the soup like it is a lucky dip and finally up comes up the jackpot and his eye is sitting on the end of the spoon, and he looks at me and laughs victoriously, "There's the little bastard." And he proceeds to stick it in his mouth to suck the soup off, take it out, rubs it on his dirt oily boiler and stick it back in black empty socket. And looks at me with this one left false glass eye glaring at me like a bulging frog's eye, "What do ya think," he said looking at me, "Good as new."

"You look great," I sort of said, "I can see you are busy, so I'll leave you to keep an eye on things," and I walked out pissing myself with laughter.

"I'll be dishing up soon," said the cook, "Don't be late or it'll get cold."

"I'm looking forward to it," I said and he smiled not catching the sarcasm in my voice. "Good Lad." And I was gone back on deck.

Tea-time arrived and the three Marx Brothers where tucking into the soup like tramps fighting over a British rail Sandwich, unable to resist I asked Ron how the soup was and he broke off from dunking his mouldy bread, cupped his hand to his ear and said, "Say again son?"

"Never mind Ron," I just couldn't do this anymore. I'll have to try semaphore.

So, turning to "Coat Hanger George" another member of our motley crew and so nick named because he looked like he still had a coat hanger in the back of his filthy shirt. "How's the soup?"

"A drop of good stuff," he answered almost spitting the contents of his mouth all over me and he started dunking his bread again and stuffing it into his mouth and churning it around his open mouth like the ships rubbish grinder.

"Are you having some son," says the cook.

"Err, no thanks." And I made my excuses, "I've got to keep an eye on the moorings, enjoy your soup," and I left the group of little piglets slurping it up. And went up top to take the first watch in the wheelhouse. Now don't get me, I've done some dangerous trips on trawlers and in the merchant navy but I had a feeling I was taking my life in my hands crossing the North Sea rust bucket.

The wind was starting blow up outside and just to point out some minor details, there were no windows left in the wheelhouse and the lights kept flashing on and off and ships generator made a sound like "Huble bubble toil and trouble" and would like make this odd bubbling sound and then a Chuga, chugga type sound. It was quite a catchy rhythm and I almost danced out the engine room doing a Rumba. Yes, I was having second thoughts and was beginning to wonder if three hundred quid was going to be worth this epic voyage of freaks. I was beginning to know how Christopher Columbus felt now and if anything was going to sail off the edge of the world it would be this ship.

The next morning, we made readied for sea. The ship was a total museum piece with hand steering. I took the wheel and the "crew" mustered on deck. I popped my head through one of the broken windows from the bridge and shouted to George. "Cast off aft, then cast off forward!!" And George is looking up me from the deck like I am talking Chinese. "Is that the back or the front."

"Are you fucking kidding me, or what?!" I shouted.

"I'm only asking," George takes on all indignant, "No need to get your knickers in a twist."

What the fuck had I got my myself into here. I couldn't be bothered to argue anymore. I just wanted get home in one. And so I gave the order again. "Cast at the front, and cast off at the back." And suddenly I had action stations, or so I thought and slowly we started to slip out moorings and I stepped back and let the Dutch pilot takes us out port. The Dutch pilot seemed breath a sigh of relief when the Pilot boat came to take him off the ship. I escorted him to the rope ladder and he scrambled over the side at some speed but not before shaking my hand and saying rather ominously I thought. "Good luck, you are going to need it." Nothing like negative vibes I thought to myself. But at least we were out into the open sea now and and it was a big wide open space, and we had no radar and only crew look outs to avoid hitting anything. By this time Captain Alcopops was in the Wheel house and he didn't look sober. He even had a old worn out Trinity House merchant navy Captain's hat on, but it might fool the crew but gave me little faith. "Right I said," raring to go, "Where's the charts and I'll plot the course." The Captain just looked at me all glassy eyed and swaying. "What charts?" he drunkenly answered.

"Like, the navigation charts," I said at him, and he just shrugged his shoulders.

"How the fuck do we get to Goole," I said at him. And just like that, the Captain went glazed, sort of went into a drunken trance and just keeled over and hit the deck with thud. By this George was on the bridge. "Take the wheel!" I shouted at him. And I went to help the captain. The bastard was out cold pissed out of his head and smelt like brewery. Suddenly I am aware the ship is lurching all over the place. I jumped up and pushed George out the way and took the wheel off him. "Have you never steered a ship?" I shouted at him. And to give him his due he answered really honestly but his answer hardly reassured me.

"No." He said simply. You don't have a ship's wheel on small barges just a hand rudder at the back.

"Just a minute," I said feeling a little uneasy. "You have sailed deep sea before haven't you." And I was about to wish I had never asked and he said that word again. "No"

I literally didn't know if I dared asked the next question. "What about the rest of the crew?" I asked ever so tentatively, "what about the rest of the crew. They have done deep sea?"

"No," and he said it again, "I mean we're only going across the North Sea. The Captain told me there was nothing to it. I know the cook had had some deep sea experience."

I pointed to the Captain laid out cold on the deck, "Well for him there is nothing to it, he was right about that." I said in panic. Something was beginning to dawn on me. I was the only deep sea seaman on this ship. And then something suddenly hit me like a 303 bullet right between the eyes. I suddenly realised that when I looked closer at the ship's compass. It didn't seem to be working properly. I mentally screamed. Even the pilot hadn't noticed. Pilot's navigate ships into and out of ports in waters known to them. By this time we couldn't even go back because it was pitch black outside and I couldn't even see the lights of Rotterdam. I mentally screamed. We were stuck out in the middle of the North Sea with no charts and a fucked compass.

"There's no fucking compass," I said aloud in panic.

"Does that matter," answered George as calm as cucumber.

"How do we get to Goole," I shouted at him, "if I don't where we are?"

George sorted stared out the bridge window and pointed, "Well it's just over there isn't it?"

I was by now panicking like mad. I knew that we had left Rotterdam sailing West but I had no idea how I was to correct the course. We could land anywhere. I started charging about like a bull in a china shop pulling draws and riffling cupboards on the bridge looking for, looking for anything.

"What you doing son?" asked George calmly.

"I need a compass, anything." I was tearing out draws and just throwing stuff around. And then George piped up. I think George has got a compass watch. Will that do?"

"Are you taking the piss or what, 'cause, you're beginning to piss me off!" I shouted at him. A minutes later the whole crew suddenly appeared on the bridge. "What the fuck are you lot doing here. Get out on deck and keep look out."

"Look out for what?" piped up the cook.

"Other fucking ships!! You idiots!"

I eventually found an old box compass in one of the cupboards and breathed a sigh of relief. Then I stuck lucky again and I found an old chart I could use after I blew the dust of it. I could at least take a good stab in the dark where I was heading and I changed course ten degrees to put on a ball park course for the mouth of the Humber. I knew the speed of the ship would take us ten hours to cross the North Sea. But I decided to slow the ship down so we would it would day light by the time we hot the UK coast and would then navigate by sight. I was beginning to settle in my own that things would be all right and I made the sign of the cross and touched and by the time cook had come back up. "Can you steer a ship?" I said at him.

"Course I can." He answered as though I had insulted.

"Well just take the wheel, don't move it. I need a piss, I'll be straight back."

I was only taking a piss over the side on deck and the ship is floundering from side to side. I ended up pissing all down my trousers and rushed back to the bridge and I turned on him, "What fucking ships have you been on, you can't steer, your way to the Bar in an empty pub."

Yes, I can, I've been on lots." he snapped back. "Well I used to help unload barges, fucking barges and did a bit on coasters."

"But have you ever been deep sea before?" I shouted at him. After a short silence, he said, "but my Dad was a coal miner, and always wanted to go to sea, but couldn't, so he told me to follow my dreams."

I stood looking with my mouth open, I was totally shocked. "A fucking coal miner and follow your dreams. Are you fucking kidding me? This is a fucking nightmare. Now get down below and send somebody up who can steer and I don't mean the ship's cat. I need someone with a brain."

Next up to the bat was 'Coat Hanger George". "Please tell me you can steer a ship," I was almost pleading with him.

"No worries there son," he answered stoutly, "My Dad taught me," he announced proudly."

"Did he go to sea then?" I asked.

"Not really," he said he was a was a window cleaner.

"A window cleaner," I answered back. This was becoming even more confusing. "Ok so who the fuck, taught him then." I was just being a nosey bastard now. But it passed the time.

"Well," he carried on, "he had a brother who was the other son of my Grandma and he went to sea."

This whole trip is getting to be one big joke. So I say to myself, calm down.

Terry, just calm down. Take a big deep breath and just calm down. I think, "ok, ok enough is enough. I can do this." I've got a compass of sorts, a chart, I can do this. I turned to this bloke, "Look just forget I ever asked. Just go and join the others and keep a look out. And if you see any other ships don't forget to come and tell me will you." I said sarcastically.

My plan to wait for day light worked and my course turned out to be good and by daylight I was approaching the Humber. It had been one hell of a long night I can tell you. By the time the pilot cam on board I was so relieved to hand it over to him and he took us safely Goole. Against all odds we had made it. I grabbed my gear and made my way down the gangplank. The Captain had sobered up and was on the quay side exchanging hand shakes and pleasantries with the new owner.

"A good job done," said the owner to the Captain.

"That's what I get paid for," answered the Captain. "A piece of cake getting her across." I felt like going up the Captain and sticking the nut on him I can tell you.

"It's all in day's work," the Captain said back to owner kissing his arse.

Before I lost my rag listening to this crap, I went up and asked for my cash and the Captain slapped it in my hand. I counted it. "There's only £250 here." I said staring hard him down. "We agreed £300." And I hell out my hand for the rest and I think my attitude sent a clear message I wanted my money. And without further a do he slapped another 5 tenners in my hand and I walked away. The Captain called after me. "You don't fancy working for me do you son?"

Well after thinking about for all of a micro second, I replied simply by saying, "No offence Captain. I don't mind a laugh and a joke but fuck a pantomime."

"Is that a no then," asked the Captain. I slung my kit over my shoulder, "YOU MUST BE FUCKING JOKING!" I laughed out loud and I headed for the hills.

It wasn't long before I got a job offer from Weston Shipping of London, the sun-bless bread company, who also owned a small fleet of modern ships and to be honest I was very happy. I worked for them for about two years and during that time it leads me to the doors of Jeanette Charles (the then official Queen of famous lookalike celebreties). And believe it or not it led me on another spin off career as a Rod Stewart look-a-like, but that's for another book that will be coming out soon.

THE SPANISH CHICKEN

We had just finished a six-month contract, running from Belfast to Antwerp. When we received some welcoming news, we had a cargo of stone chippings to take to a small port in Spain called Pasajes. We made our way to Cornwall to load at a place called Stone quarry (how very original). Anyway, whilst the scenery was beautiful, the same could not be said for the place we were to load, which was a right shit hole. A heavy sea swell was throwing the ship up and down and it very dangerous. After several nerve wracking hours, we were finally loaded and on our way. The voyage to Spain was not without incident, as we were crossing the Bay of Biscay we hit a big storm. It was like being in a giant washing machine, which prompted me to make a poem, lest I should forget that trip.

> Onwards and onwards through the swirling storm
>
> We battered our way, from dusk to dawn
>
> No quarter given, no quarter ask

Just how much longer

Would this storm last

A break from the wind

A lull from the swell

An answer that only nature could tell

Onwards and onwards through this stormy hell!

Ooh, I was a poet and didn't know it

Now back to the story. We finally arrived at Pasajes, which had a narrow entrance flanked by what appeared to be two medieval forts, I was quite impressed by its innocent beauty. Well we duly moored up alongside the quay. As it was late afternoon and Thursday, we were given another bonus in the shape of, we could not discharge cargo until the Tuesday, due to the fact that there would not be any mobile grabs available until then, because it was basically a small fishing village and the mobile grabs were the only equipment they had for unloading cargo. Also, there was going to be some sort of festival taking place over the weekend. Result, on the Saturday we were sat in the recreation room having a beer or three, as you do.

Any we are sitting having a beer blast and the cook came in. As you may have guessed I like to give nick names, it's a Hull thing. Everybody gets a nick name in Hull or they just use your surname with an addition. Like my name in Hull amongst mates, is Coxy. Since I'm from Hull I gave very body a nick name and the cook was no exception I called him Alf because he was a dead ringer for Alfred Hitchcock, but smaller and fatter. I mean he was a good bloke and an exceptionally good "pan artist" (a good cook). So he comes in he sits down and got a beer, then said, "Will you do me a favour?" Jokingly I said, "If its money or beer you want, no problem, but if you want me to fix you up with one of the local senoritas, I don't do miracles you ugly bastard."

"Piss off!" he jokingly hit back, "no nothing like that, I was going to do roast chicken for Sunday dinner and I've only got one chicken, I forgot to order more,"

"So how do I come into the picture then?" I asked, "Who do think I am Old McDonald." Although I already had a notion what was coming next.

We were moored alongside the quay just inside the dock entrance. And as is the case in a lot of small ports on the continent, there was a small holding running alongside the dock and it just so happened that this one had quite a few chickens.

"Well," said the cook winking and going all artful. "You just over to the small holding and nick a few chickens."

"Do your own dirty work," I answered back. "Move ya arse and nick them yourself."

The cook sort of mocked his less than athletic portly figure. "Oh come on Coxy, jus look at me. I aren't exactly built for chasing chickens around. You're only a young pup." And he winked back. "I'll owe you one."

I sighed and looked at the crew sat around drinking beer. "We'll see what we can do eh lads. Leave it with us. "

As the weather was hot, very hot we decided to have a couple more liquid libations whilst I formulated the daring raid on the Spanish chicken coup. After some serious drunken deliberations, we decided to use the trusted two, four, two as formation, but as there were only four of us, we concluded that it might not work. So as a sub defuse we decided to just have a kick about with a football, and the ball would get "accidentally" kicked over the the fence that separated the quay side from this small holding and then nab the chickens. It would be piece of cake. By this time, it was late afternoon, when our look out reported that the old doddery Spanish protector of the small holding had mounted his motorised trolley and was heading for the Tavern and the festivities to blow his brains out on Spanish plank. It was zero hour and time to put our master plan into action. So having changed into our England strip, jeans and work boots (well we were sailors not footballers) we emerged onto the hallowed turf, or in this case gravely quayside and started belting the ball about. I quickly spotted a likely looking pair of birds of the chicken variety I might add in the "visitors end of the stadium". They would look good surrounded by three veg and a couple of Yorkshire puddings I thought to my self. The whistle went and we kicked off, and horror of horrors, someone "accidentally" kicked the ball over the fencing and it was action stations. We all bolted and shimmied over the fence. I thought it would have been easy, but, these old broilers were no sitting ducks. In fact, they were like that cartoon character, The Road Runners on steroids. We just couldn't catch the little bastards and they were running rings around us. After about twenty minutes of ducking and diving we all regrouped heaving and panting our lungs up.

"This is no good," I said coughing my lungs up, "we needed a change of tactics."

"Let's come back later," said 'Pizza Face' the deck hand, almost heaving his last breath.

"Good idea." I conceded huffing and chuffing. "We'll regroup to the mess and make a second assault after dark. They'll be roosting by then."

"I'm looking forward to ringing their bleedin' necks," growled 'Pizza Face', "the bloody run around they've just given us."

So we retreated back to the ship in disgrace having been turned over by a couple of chickens. I was steaming hot and I was sweating like a little piggy. Time for a, shit, shower and a shave, before heading into the town for a bit of sun, sea, sangria, and Senoritas and hopefully bit of Spanish "rumpy pumpy". Once, we were all suited, booted, with splash of cheap after shave and togged up with a pack of six Durex each (ever the optimist that's me, wink, wink), which were free from the dispensary, off we went having previously front loading with duty free booze on board. But not before Alf the cook stopped me for an update as regards Sunday dinner, "Don't worry Alf," I assured him, "I have a cunning plan, just chill out and leave it with us." and off we toddled in the direction of the lights and sound of Spanish dancing musica.

It was only about a ten-minute walk and when we got there I was a little surprised how busy it was. The festival was in full swing. Everyone was dressed in their finery and national costume's; I must admit the women looked good in their colourful flamenco dresses. There was this big stage in the middle of the festival with this guitarist strumming like a mad man with some Spanish Lolita's giving it loads clattering their feet doing this mad Flamenco as only Spanish birds know how, and then would do a swirl and their skirts would rise up to show their little black frilly knickers and after a couple weeks at sea this did not help matters in the old "boiler room" department if you get my drift. 'Pizza Face' almost had his tongue hanging out watching with bulging eyes. Anyway I dragged him away and it didn't take long to sniff out the biggest and best tavern. Mainly because there was only one, but not to be put off, it was onwards and upwards. We thought a while looking at this dump that passed for a bar and duly entered said watering hole. And as we went inside, I couldn't help but feel the only thing missing was the theme tune from the Good, Dad and the Ugly as all eyes were on the Gringos who had just walked in. I half expected Clint Eastwood and Lee Van Cleef to jump out any moment and start blasting. It resembled one of those outback wild west saloons you find in Spaghetti Westerns but not as clean and with the usual Spanish tradition of hanging up road kill was evident all around. We slowly moseyed up to the bar and this big fat Spanish barman in a Sombrero slowly asked, "Ci Senoirs," and gave us the evil eye, which I kindly polished for him, before handing it back. He was stood polishing a filthy glass, with an even filthier rag. Which I assumed could have been one of his dad's old vests. It was hard to tell if the mucky bastard had stubble or a swarm of midget flies an around his chin. "You want crevasse", he hissed through blackened teeth that reminded me of a grave yard full of old broken head stones. Wiping away the spittle that he had just showered us with, we said "Ci senor", which was about my limit when it came to our Spanish. And he plonked three bottles of beer onto the bar, "You want glass?" he asked. But fearing we might catch some as yet undiscovered diseases from his jam jars that he passed as glasses, I smiled. "It's OK." And we declined the offer and found a quiet corner in which to take in the ambience of this bordello. I couldn't help but feeling a little uneasy, especially as the "Spanish Rigsby" behind the bar kept glaring at us, maybe it was because he was not used to seeing clean humans in this dos house. It mattered not as the stale mate was broken by the arrival of a hoard of festival goers bursting in through the bat wing doors. All of them dressed in their very fine costumes, among them where a couple of tasty looking senoritas. It didn't take them long to spot the Gringo's in the corner. One of them seemed to know "Spanish Rigby" behind the bar rather well. I could not figure out whether she was his wife, daughter or grand-daughter. To my surprise she came over and in quite good English asked if she could join us. "Absolutely !!" I blurted out. She looked stunning in her blue flamenco dress so much so, I thought I was in the sub-marine service as my periscope started to rise in my pants. We got chatting and she told us her Mother was English, who met her Dad when he was a waiter (no surprise there then).

Anyway, the good news was the "Spanish Rigsby" barman was no relation and who by now was looking at me with daggers. Now I don't know where he got his beer from, but it was going right through me and I had to go and stroke the swan's neck. Fortunately, the toilet was cleaner than the bar and once I had raised the water level by a couple of inches, I tapped the drops off on the heel of my shoes. As you would expect from someone as modest as myself, as I descended out of the depositary, who should be stood there, but Isabelle, the Dago bird from the bar and before I could speak, she stuck the plunger kiss on me, like with such Spanish fire like she had never kissed anyone before. Well that was it for me, the old passion probe was throbbing and ready to leave the launch pad. So I pulled her into the toilet and we got down to business fast, furious and within seconds her flamenco skirt was up round her waist and with no tights to fumble around with, and her black nickers so skimpy, removal was not needed and next I we were bouncing each other off the small bog closet walls in an urgent frenzy for the next ten to fifteen minutes and both of us fell into each others arms breathing heavy as the urgency suddenly left us both, and the deed was done and we were both well satisfied customers. After both our bolts had been shot, she threw her arms around my neck and that's when the horror hit me as her arm pits looked like the hanging gardens of Babylon, but I had done my bit for Queen and country and shown the flag. Job done I thought, and isn't it just so strange how after you have your wicked way with a girl, you realise how fucking ugly they really are and that the beauty you fooled yourself into seeing was no more than the urging in your pants playing tricks on you. A bit like dying of thirst in a desert and you see a mirage of that paradise watering hole.

I tried as discreetly as I could not to let my lost enthusiasm show and casually returned to my shipmates with modesty still intact. But they were grinning all over their faces like daft little kids. Little did I know that my zip was open and when Isabella followed a little moment later looking all innocent, though flushed with satisfaction she had the back of her skirt stuck in knickers with the buttocks of her big arse smiling at every body. Given the circumstances, I don't think the situation had gone un-noticed, as the "Spanish Rigsby" behind the bar was looking at me like someone had just stuffed a cactus up his arse. Despite getting the evil eyes off the rest off the patrons, the night fortunately passed off without any ugly scenes or me getting my head bashed by the local Dagoes for banging one of their local innocent virgins – I don't think so. Anyway the night wore on, the drinks slid down in great abundance and Isabell started to look gorgeous again. And suddenly out of nowhere some non descript Spanish bloke just produced this guitar and started violently strumming some Spanish folk tune and singing like a midnight moggy that had got it's balls caught in a rabbit snare. What is it about the Spanish? This Spanish guitar bloke almost had sparks coming off the guitar and suddenly the Spanish lasses were up almost instantly and clattering their maracas and stamping their feet and giving it loads with skirts swishing up and again knickers in view everywhere and so close to us dancing that their little tight bums were almost in our faces. But I have to admit it was a sight to behold and Isabelle and her Spanish female friends treated us to a faultless flamenco dance. And by this time my boiler was lit again and with a wink to Isabelle I went to bogs again closely followed by my Spanish nympho and it wasn't long before we were both at it for round two. What a fucking night!

It was the early hours of the morning before people started to drift off home, so we decided to call it a night and head back to the ship. I still had Isabell hanging onto my arm and after a big drunken sloppy snog I arranged to meet up her the next night. When I thought about, whilst the face left a bit to be desired, the body was amazing, and as they say in Hull, "You don't look at the mantle piece when you're poking the fire." And hopefully she might shave her arm pits by then.

So with my ship mates we staggered back signing, "Whiskey in the jar O'" and was just about to go up the gang plank when another one of the lads, nick named 'Harpic" because he drives everyone around the bend. "Just a minute!" he blurted out, "What about Alf's chickens?'

We all looked at each other through our drunken haze with the full on bravado. "Let's go fucking show them chickens lads!" I said steely eyed. "let's show them chickens who's boss."

But fear not as luck was on our side, because Alf's cabin was facing the quayside and because it was a warm night the little fat fucker had his port hole open. We carefully snuck up and we could hear him snoring, which meant he had been on the piss and was sleeping it off. And not even an atomic bomb going off would wake him up.

We were over the fence and in no time and quickly had the chickens by legs who were in the coup roosting. They didn't stand a chance in our surprise attack and clucking and wings flapping we scrambled back over the fence and onto the quay side

Then with the dexterity of a silent S.A.S. commando, laughing and giggling we eased the two squawking chickens through Alf's open port hole and crept back aboard like midnight burglars and hit our bunks, and what with all the Spanish plonk, I went out like a light. It only seemed like I was in the land of nod for five minutes and all hell was breaking loose and I looked at my bedside clock and I had been spark out for four hours and all I could hear was, "COCKA-DOODLE DOO!!"

"What the fuck!" I said aloud and was out my pram and in the gangway and followed the racket to Alf's cabin. The rest of crew were now up and outside Alf's cabin too. And again came a big, "COCKADOODLE DOO!" coming from behind Alf's cabin door and somebody was clearly falling about in there judging from the ruckas. I opened the door and what a sight, there was chicken shit and feathers everywhere, including on Alf's head. It turned out one of the chickens wasn't a chickens at all, it was a bloody rooster and gave us all the dawn chorus. Also, it must have taken umbrage at Alf and thought he was trying it on with one of his hens. So the rooster had taken drastic measures to teach Alf a lesson, and Alf was laid on his back on the cabin floor, still half pissed with this Rooster at on his chest head butting Alf.

The poor sod his face looked like a well-used dart-board. "How did they get in?" he drunkenly protested. And as quick as a fart, I simply said "Oh come on Alf, don't tell me you left your port-hole open again?" Looking all confused, sheepish and covered in chicken shit, he carried on, "Well it was hot and I couldn't sleep."

"Well there you go then," I said artfully giving a wink to the lads, "they were most likely looking for somewhere to roost and seeing an opening invited themselves in for a bit of a kip."

"Yeah," protested Alf, "but look at the fucking mess. Come on lads, help me clean up."

It was the signal to bolt, "Good night Alf!" we all answered in a chorus and we beat a hasty retreated back to our pits and the land of nod.

I must have been out for a few hours as the sun was well up when I stirred into motion. After a quick shower, I got dressed and went into the mess room, Harpic was sat there grinning like a manic.

"What's wrong with you." I said at him.

"The skipper wants a word with you." was the reply.

"Oh fuck, don't tell me he knows about last night? I said apprehensively.

"No, no," retorted Harpic, "he's blaming Alf for being stupid enough to leave his port-hole open."

"Thank fuck for that." Then speak of the Devil and he appears, and Captain appeared and like I said earlier, we had a good crew and that included the skipper.

"Ah! Terry, just the man I want to see you,"

"Oh shit!" I thought to myself and I feared the worst.

"I take it you heard all the commotion this morning."

"Yes skipper," I answered all innocent.

"Apparently," said the Skipper, "the cook in his infinite wisdom left his port-hole open and some of the local wild life invited themselves in."

"Yes Captain," I answered all formal and slightly grovelling, and added then added some humour to my voice. "I've just had a word with him about that and it seems he lost a fight with some chicken stowaways." And I couldn't help a snigger of laughter, "Have you seen his face captain?"

"Mmm, yes," answered the Captain, "I have indeed, not a pretty sight, I thought we had an out- break of chicken pox aboard if you pardon the pun." Thinking that was the best one liner in history, the Captain started to laugh like a howling monkey. Out of polite- ness we all joined in. But its wasn't that funny, but after all he was the Captain.

"But that's not what I want to speak to you about," the Captain suddenly changed the subject, "I take it you had a goodnight ashore last night?" he enquired.

I knew what was coming and knew it involved money. Seizing the initiative, I started to plead poverty. "It would have been better if it wasn't for the lack of funds captain."

"Quit right, quit right," said the Captain stoutly. "Unfortunately you had already gone ashore, when the ships agent arrived with the local currency. I've given the rest of the crew a sub on their wages. I take it you would like one as well?"

"Well that's very kind of you captain." I was grovelling again, "yes please". What he didn't know was that one of the lads had been to Spain on his last trip and had a wad of pesetas, to fund our night ashore.

Well," said the Captain, "come to my cabin and sign for it if you would."

I didn't need asking twice. I signed on the dotted line and was all set for my lustful night out with Isabella and more assignation.

I thought I would pay a curtesy visit on Alf in his culinary laboratory (galley). He was busy cooking up another delectable delicacy. "Fuck me Alf, what's that stink?" I asked grinning. Cook's get endless stick at sea and are the butt of endless jokes and wind ups about their cooking. But it was all good humoured and knew how to give as good as he got. He lifted the lid on a whacking great pan and there doing a pathetic imitation of a drowning duck, where his two pets from the night before.

"I told you I would sort the fuckers out," he proudly announced. "Vengeance is a dish best ate cold, but I thought I'd make an exception with these two little fuckers."

"Nice one Alf." I said, "I'll leave you to it then, while your finalising your recipe for a Michelin star. " and I was out the door, "By the way Alf," I said turning, "you want to put some suntan lotion on your noggin , your head looks like a fucking pumpkin."

"Do us a favour Coxy will ya?

"What's that Alf?"

Piss off! And lose the door behind you before you get my boot up your arse," he retorted with a friendly laugh. And I was gone.

The rest of the day was pretty much uneventful, except for Alf's Sunday dinner. It was pretty much what I was expecting, the over boiled chicken tasted worse than it smelled and road kill sprang to mind. Alf assured everyone that it would taste better with a bit of seasoning. I informed him that it had dead for all the four seasons. However, I was willing to give him the benefit of the doubt, so I added a bit of seasoning, in the form of salt, pepper, tobacco sauce, mint jelly, horse radish, sauce, chilli flakes and apple sauce, or a splash of toilet cleaner, but alas it was all in vain, because it still tasted, fucking horrible.

I just mooched about for the rest of the day before it was time to head for town and my much-anticipated meeting with Isabella. I even put on a clean pair of undies (well I wanted to make a good impression) and off I went with the same motley crew from last night. I don't know if it was us being a bit paranoid or what. But we got the distinct impression that the locals looked very suspicious of us, especially, those working on the small holding near the ship and when we walked passed one of them, he angrily held out this pitch fork and sort of dug out in our direction and spit at the floor landing this great green medallion near my feet and they all gave us a glare of anger and started ranting in Spanish. Now I don't speak Spanish, but a rough translation might be something along the lines of, "Filthy English. Gringo, pigs, stealers of prize winning chickens. Who come here with no respect, no money and take advantage of our women." or words to that effect, well our shoulders were broad and apart from the gringo pigs, he seemed to know us quite well. Yes, I had to admit this Spanish bloke was quite a good judge of character.

We duly arrived at the one star taverna also, we had nick named "Rigsby's Bordello," but our high spirits and happy mood was about to be shattered. As we entered said establishment. We were confronted by this rather irate looking Spanish bloke who promptly reached under his sterile bar top and produced what looked like a rusty old gun from the Napoleonic wars and jabbed it in the direction of the door. Big mistake. The filthy fool obviously didn't know who he was dealing with. We were proud English sea faring warriors of the old school. My grand Dad had been at The Somme and I had relatives that had landed at Dunkirk and with that blood in me I didn't frighten easily. It took us all of a second before we were in self defence mode and we were in full retreat backwards and legged it up the road in great haste. I later sus-pected that he had somehow found out that I had banged a bird in his bog, or maybe he had just trapped his todger in his flies, but we didn't hang around to find out. I just hope that the shame he thought we had brought on his village would one day prove too much and someone would go into the bog only to be confronted by a pair of legs sticking out of the pan with "Rigsby" having topped himself leaving traumatized locals annoyed at him for not completely flushing bog afterwards.

We found ourselves in the position of being up the creek without a paddle and still had three days in port but did not venture into the village as Spanish vendetta had been made against us. And the moral of the story is when you're up to your neck in shit, keep your mouth shut and don't push your luck. And thankfully by the time we sailed I found no horses head in my bed.

Anyway our way back to the ship, still with great haste, we were thrown an unexpected life-line in the shape of this witchy looking Spanish peasant type old hag. She was beckoning us to go down a side street, being the eternal optimist, Harpic pointed out that it might be a trap and we could get ambushed. I reassuringly in-formed him that in the very unlikely event of that happening, all we had to do was shout Nelson and Trafalgar, that would send the unwashed hoards quickly heading for the hills.

As it turned out our concern about ending up in concrete wellies and being thrown into the dock was totally unfounded. We chanced it and we followed the old hag down the narrow alleyway and she turned into another side street and to our pleasant sur-prise it was very busy with the festival goers. She pointed to a door and it was a tapas-bar. Far better and cleaner than "Rigsby" tavern and proven by the fact it had clean sawdust on the floor, and there wasn't a pair of stained underpants or smelly socks hung up with the dried road kill and chipolatas.

Now when it came to women in foreign ports I have my standards. But sad to say not all the members of the crew had such discerning choice as me when it came to women. And as far as my ship mate Harpic was concerned he too had standards when it came to the foreign ladies who tend to hang around foreign ports. And one of them was they had to be under seven feet tall, other than that Harpic thought they were fair game. And sorry to say Harpic pulled the old hag and money changed hands, and ten minutes after disappearing upstairs Harpic was back down stairs with a big smile of self satisfaction on his face and the rest of us just looked at each other and cringed.

"Oh well," I thought philosophically to my self, "It takes all sorts make a world." But it would be several weeks later that Harpic was pissing razor blades and it meant a trip to the knob doctor and a couple of injections in the arse.

We after an uneventful night we headed for back to base. I decided it would be the better part of valour when I got back to the ship to stay on board for the rest of our docking. Mainly better for my health mainly. And sadly, I never got to see the little Spanish nymphet Isabella again. When the time came and we weighed anchor sailed out of port, thankfully with all crew intact and never did darken that Spanish port again. Though I would never forget our visit and as for Isabella, she become just another name to add to my growing list of ladies of every nationality I would 'bump' into on my worldly travels. And by this time I was missing home and England was calling and I was sure I could smell the green, green grass of home.

Whilst many seamen will tell you that life at sea was mundane, there were many times that were funny and stood out. I will try to concentrate on them. I remember one occasion when I found myself in Singapore and my ship was in dry dock, we were in a place up the river in the Jungle at a place called Samba Wan

Anyway a few of us went ashore for a night out and the there was only one establishment that passed as a bar in the village. Truth be known it was nothing more than a huge shack, with three or four wooden barrels and a couple of planks of wood for the bar. So anyway we are set out with beer a plenty and all is well with the world. But there is always someone or something that pisses on your bonfires. So we are minding our own business and a group of Anzac Soldiers came in giving it the big bravado. Now one of our stewards was seeing a local girl but what none of us knew was that she was also seeing one of these soldiers.

I suppose the outcome was inevitable and as they often say in newspapers, "A scuffle broke out." And soon chairs and tables were flying all over the place and it had turned into full on a room brawl. I could hear the crack of chins and noses being broken and there was blood and snot spilling all over the place. Me and my mate was stood at the end of the bar, enjoying the evening's entertainment, when one of these arse-holes came flying towards us on the end of a sucker punch from one of our lads. We simply lifted our beer up and moved aside and he landed on the deck. But this Anzac quickly got up and was about to re-join the punch up and my mate just smashed this bottle over head. Unfortunately for my mate this Anzac was huge and the bottle seemed no more than irritant and he just turned round picked up my mate and sent him flying through the air like a trapeze artist and landed with a big thump behind the bar.

Now not only were these Anzacs huge they outnumbered us as well and this Anzac then homed in on another ship that was behind me- the one he thought was shagging his bird and he started to rush by me and I decided to even things up a bit as he ran by, I stuck my foot out and he ended up using his face for a brake and my ship mate was on him like a shot and throwing in punches and flying kicks as this bloke lay on the floor. The next thing, a bottle flew by me and twatted my mate on the head, "That's it!" he screamed at the top of voice and he started pitching punches like a Tasmanian Red Devil. Wham! Bang! thank you Mam and he floored three out in no time. Another tried to club from behind with a broken chair leg. But my mate was onto him and I grabbed the chair leg and belted him with all might with it. By now the Anzacs were retreating out the doors and we chased them chased him outside. I was in full Hessle Road fighting mode and I bolted outside throwing caution to the wind. But in my haste I forgot about one thing, the monsoon ditch outside and the bloke I was chasing jumped over it and I didn't with the result I ended up in the bottom the bottom of this deep ditch up to my neck in mud.

After it all blow over we headed for town but not before licking our wounds and getting cleaned up. Its then that my pint-sized pocket battleship of a mate confessed, that before joining the merchant navy he was the boxing champ of the royal navy. How they got a boxing ring on a sub I will never know.

The next day I woke up with the pain of all pains in my foot, it was black and blue. I was duly dispatched to hospital, where I was told it was broken and my trip was over. I was kept in and while I was there some of the crew came to visit bringing with them a case of beer which was deposited under my bed. We were having a laugh and a joke when one of the lads looked at the bloke in next Bed, ere that's the bloke who started the fight last night he said, and so it was. He had a broken leg, and realising the cat was out of the bag he started shouting for the nurse, "Sod that!" one of the lads piped up and picked up a walking stick and hit him on his pot leg.

The nurse was soon on the scene, "What's going on?" she asked.

"He's having a fit," I said joking and before we knew it he was getting a sedative. Then a quack arrived and spotted the beer under the bed and believe it or not he was from Hull and he looked at me and said, "You're a trouble maker, I can always tell." And he pointed into my face. "You are out of here in six days my lad." I was god smacked, me, a trouble maker?

I spent the next five days there before I was discharged, and flown home just in time for Christmas. Because my foot was in plaster the airport checking counter assistant in all her wisdom seated me in the middle of four seats in the centre aisle on this Jumbo jet.

But once again fortune seemed to be smiling on me, in the shape of a rather buxom middle aged Dutch lady, who took it upon herself to be my personal nurse. And whilst it was a very busy and long flight back to the UK, it was made more pleasant by having all the attention of said lady.

Looking back on it, I thought if I had not been incapacitated I would have paid her kindness back by introducing her to some bedroom Olympics in nearby hotel on landing. Or that might have just been wishful thinking on my behalf. I will never know. But what I did know was that no matter who you are, or where you come from there are still some decent people out there willing to help others less fortunate than themselves shall we say.

Chair up Albo was his name.

There was another funny story I remember with mirth; I was working for a Norwegian deep sea diving shipping company where I had three golden years.

One time I had just got home on leave when I got a call asking me if I would join another ship. Just for a week to cover for someone who had a death in the family. Of course I said I would. The ship was at anchor just off the Humber waiting for the next job and so I went to Grimsby where I caught the pilot boat to take me to the ship. As I knew most of the crew I soon settled in. The skipper was called fat Nick for obvious reasons he was a big fat smelly lazy bastard, who thought we were all his personal man servants.

As I said I knew most of the crew from other ships I had sailed on and we all got on like proverbial house on fire. I was the Boson in charge of the deck department, and each morning I would go on the bridge for work orders for the day. The the first mate would go and call out fat nick, who always took the day watch 8-4 and he would always wait till the last minute to then come up to the bridge. If he could get away with dodging a minute of work, he would. I thought I was a lazy bastard but this bloke even put me to shame.

He always had a plate of bacon sandwiches and a mug of tea at 8-30am because he was too lazy to go down to the mess-room for breakfast. The next day saw us heading back to Grimsby to put the cook ashore as he had an accident (we suspected the pig he was preparing for nick's breakfast had bitten him) but nothing was proved. Also Captain Nick had a very annoying habit of chewing something that wasn't there. So he always looked like a camel chewing the cud. So the whole crew decided to Christen him Albert Cud.

 After changing the cooks over we returned to anchor, the new cook was called Steve who I knew and although he may have been young, he was quite a good cook. Unfortunately for him, he was also very gullible, and easy to wind up. Once he had settled in he came into the mess-room, seeking out the usual information, like: "What was the crew like?" "Who was the skipper..." etc. Now I had primed him I told him Fat Nicks breakfast routine, and that his name was Albert cud and that after he got to know him, he could call him Albo, but if he was in bad mood to call him Cudy .

Well this day had started like one of those days were no one could do right as far as Fat Nick was concerned. And so in the afternoon he called me onto the bridge to read me the riot act for not on turning the crew to work on time I couldn't believe it, they were five bloody minutes late. Well I thought I would teach the bastard a lesson. One of his habits was to wedge his fat carcass into his swivel chair and spin it around. It made a real noisy squeak but he wouldn't have it oiled in case someone else sat in it, then he would hear it. So, the next morning I went onto the bridge to get the day's work list and while the mate went to call Cudy, I un-screwed his chair to just the last couple of threads. Anyway Cudy came up, I went down and waited. Steve took his breakfast ham-per up and he came back down and as we were having a yarn the tannoy squawked into life. It was the second engineer on the bridge, "Bosun Cox come to the bridge quick!" It sounded like a flap was on and the last words over the tannoy were, "The skip-pers ooh nice..." and it all went quiet. Well me, Steve and a deck-hand rushed up onto the bridge and there was fat nick rolling about on the floor firmly wedged in his seat, all purple faced and screaming obscenities at us, "Don't just stand there fucking gawk-ing," he shouted writhing about on the floor stuck in this chair and he shouted, "Get me out of this chair!" And looking straight at poor Steve he accused Steve, "You did this. I know you did," he said spitting blood and looking at stunned. And what came next I just couldn't believe, Steve replied, "Calm down Albo," he said, "I don't know what you're on about,"

It was time for stage two of the plan. We all wanted revenge, so we deliberately messed about pretending to pull and tug. After a few minutes, I said, "Hold on lads this isn't working." So I suggested that Steve and the second engineer grab an arm each while me and the deckhand grab a leg each. So off we go and while me and the deckhand grabbed a leg each we each put one foot on the chair, except Steve decided he could get a better leverage if he put his boot on the side of Fat Nicks head. So we are in position and ready to heave at the order, "Ready?" I said to all, and I gave the order, "1,2,3 HEAVE!"

Well we heaved and pulled to the muffled screams of Cudy and a like a cork popping out of a bottle of cheap plonk he suddenly popped out and then rolled onto his hands and knees. Reluctantly we all had to help him up to his feet and by this time his face had become crimson with rage with this perfect imprint of Steve's boot on his cheek. Well he went into melt down screaming at us. "Get off my fucking bridge you bastard's! The lot of you and you!" he fumed pointing at Steve, "You! Your poor man's excuse for a pan shaker (cook)" And he walked about the bridge raging like a mad man, "Your all fucking sacked." And there was no stopping him now. "Bastards the lot of you. I know your all plotting against me, but it won't work see. I've got your cards marked."

Poor old daft lad Steve couldn't help putting his foot in it again and I couldn't believe again what he said to the Captain. Steve calmly looked at the Captain and said, "Calm down Albo and I'll make you a nice pot of tea."

"You cheeky little piss taking bastard," the Captain raged back. "fuck your tea!" he screamed and as we left the bridge he railed at Steve at the top of his voice. "My name, isn't Albo you fucking retard!" ouch!!! I silently said to my self and cringed.

Then suddenly young daft Steve started ranting back at the Captain, "Good, fuck you as well then Cuddy," yelled Steve, as we left the bridge. And the Captain was suddenly having a go at me. "And you, call yourself a fucking Bosun." he said at me, "Get that fucking anchor up, we are going to Yarmouth."

I smiled and sang a tune out loud sarcastically, "Oh I do like the sea side." And left the bridge.

We were soon on our way, and eventually docked without further incident or tantrums from Fat Nick and as for sacking us all. I guessed that would have taken some explaining and so it was just forgotten.

It was a Saturday afternoon and as Fat Nick lived locally he said he was going home for the night but not before Steve had informed him, that he wasn't going to take any more of his shit, and he too was going home. Now Cuddy knew he was in the wrong and tried to smooth things over to no avail and when Steve had gone. Cuddy came into the mess room and announced he was bringing his wife and kids down for Sunday tea,

"One of you must go cook for a couple of days." he said arrogantly.

"Well don't look at me," I retorted, "I'm going home on Monday, my jobs done." Thinking quickly, I had a dastardly plan hatching. I proposed to the Captain I may have a solution to the cook dilemma. "And what's that?" he sneered smugly back.

"Well," I said, "Whiplash (a crew member) is retiring this trip and he reckons he can shake a pan with the best of them, I'll go and get him."

Now Whiplash was a decent enough old bloke who should have swallowed the hook (anchor) and retired long ago, but the sea had been his life and he found it hard to let go. As I say he was a non-offensive nice guy, but also gullible. I found him in his cabin. I took a friendly approach, "Now then Whiplash," I said gently, "the skipper wants a word with you." We called him whiplash because the poor old sod liked certain types of porno books, if you get me drift. Also had about a dozen strands of long wispy hair on one side of this head, combed over, if the wind caught it, he would have had someone's eye out. So combining these two points, they added up to calling him Whiplash. Well it made sense to us at the times. Anyway, while he went to see the skipper, we legged it to the pub and a short time later the pub door open's and in wobbled a worried looking Whiplash, "Hey up squire," I said, "what's wrong?

"That bastard Cuddy told me I must cook the tea tomorrow for him and his fat wife and fat kids"

"Ooh nasty." we all piped up.

"I don't know fuck all about cooking," said Whiplash, "The silly bastard has got some smoked salmon wants me to cook it."

Whiplash shook his head in despair, " And I haven't got a clue how to do it."

I saw the chance for some more fun here and a bit of revenge on Cuddy.

"You stop worrying Whiplash," I reassured him, we're your mates aren't we. Well we can help you out mate."

Whiplash eyes brightened up, "Oh will ya thank lads."

"You just go get the beer in and we will discuss a plan of action." I said easily and I could see Whiplash thought all his troubles were over.

When he returned with the beer we got down to business. "Right whiplash," I said, "first we know he is a greedy pig who would eat shit if it had sugar on it."

Whiplash started mischievously giggling, "Yeah, he is a greedy bastard."

"Now don't give this too much thought because we know that this might hurt your brain." Whiplash was the type of bloke who would never know an insult if it hit in the face. "but just think about it. What is salmon?"

Whiplash though hard about my question and rubbed his chin for a moment before saying, "Well its fish ain' it?

" Well done son," I said smiling in victory. "And what does every body like with fish?"

"Mushy peas." Whiplash snapped back. This was hard going now.

"Well you're not wrong Whiplash," I answered, "But what else would you get with fish?" Whiplash was thinking hard. "I'll give you a little clue here," I teased him. "Think of what you would get with fish if you went to the fish shop?" I could almost hear Whiplash's brain ticking over and then a eureka moment, "CHIPS!" Whiplash shouted at me.

"Well done Whiplash," I said, "exactly chips."

"And I can do mushy peas as well?" said Whiplash.

"You're a fucking wonder Whiplash," I said answering his cookery genius, "It'll be a meal fit for a king."

"But how do I cook it?" Whiplashed asked with note of ignorance in his voice.

Now I can be a wicked bastard when I want. But let's go the whole hog I thought. "Just melt a bag of lard and fry a bucket of chips, stick the salmon in with chips, a few mushy peas spread over the tope and the job's a good one. A pile of bread and butter and it'll go down a treat. Just Remember keep it simple. And remember Whiplash," I cautioned him. "The skipper likes his fish in crispy batter."

"Batter?" quizzed Whiplash

"Look there ya go again Whiplash panicking!" I reassured him, "me and the lads will knock up a batch tomorrow for you, now go get some more beer in its your round. Oh, ok cheers lads and off to the bar he went and a goodnight was had by all.

The next day we sat around waiting for the pub to open but we knocked up a batch of the finest fish batter for whiplash and just before cuddy came aboard with his fat brood we legged it up the to the pub sharpish. While we were enjoying the delights of the local ales, the local arsehole strutted over and with a smug look at me said, "Hey Rod gave us a song." Now I used to get this shit everywhere I went because some would say I looked like Rod Stewart. And whilst it could be a good angle with the birds, there would always be a sarcastic bastard ready to take the mick or start trouble.

"Sure I said "how about" one from the Sparks' This town isn't big enough for the both of us, so fuck off we are busy. And you won't get your head smashed in."

It seemed like a good choice and this bloke "did one" mumbling some obscenities.

Well it wasn't long before whiplash with a turned up with a face like an undertaker having a good day. "What's up then mate?" one of the lads asked, "What's up?" Whiplash echoed, "That bastard Cuddy just sacked me and you lot as well!"

"Well he cannot sack me," I said, "because I'm only relieving, and I go home tomorrow, anyhow what have we done wrong this time?" As if we didn't know."

Whiplash looked me all mystified. "I slaved all day over that stove and all the thanks I got was he said I was trying to poison him. The ungrateful bastard said I ruined his family's tea, and I wouldn't make a cook while got a hole in my arse.

Well," I swooned, "Blow me down, the ungrateful bastard. What went wrong mate with fish and chips?" And we were all trying not to laugh but it went straight over Whiplash's head.

But poor old whiplash was nearly in tears, "Cuddy said he had never heard of anyone being stupid enough to deep fry smoked salmon."

"I tell you whiplash," I said with mocking outrage, "That man is Philistine, no taste. I mean look at his wife. Last time I saw a face like that it was being ridden on the beach in the donkey derby,"

"Yeah," retorted Whiplash, "She is fucking ugly. I have some birds across the world in my time. But I never had so much booze I could wake up to that on the pillow next to me."

And that's the end of this little ditty. Oh, well who said a life on the ocean waves was plain sailing, roll on tomorrow. In the words of a Rod Stewart song, "I'm going home!"

WILD TIMES IN THE SEVENTIES

In the seventies and eighties, it was widely known in foreign port's that British ships always carried alcohol and for places such as Scandinavia they were a magnet for the local totty, who were after a free piss up. Unlike the U.K. where we have pubs and night clubs and took for granted it would be the same anywhere. Sad to say in these countries they were pretty much non-existent.

It was on one such occasion I found myself on a ship heading for Sweden. Yes, I can hear all you dirty buggers out there say, Sweden. The land of pornography, blond leggy Viking beauties all gagging for it. Well that what they said in all those Swedish porno mags I read at sea on those long lonely nights in my bunk doing stuff I am not going to tell you about.

Anyway we docked on a Friday afternoon and knew we would not be loading cargo until Monday. So, if the ships safety was kept, those who were not watch-keeper had the weekend off. Well the local jungle drums must have been working overtime. And as it was only a small port in a small town so it wasn't long before the local birds started to beat a track to the ship. We believed in sharing, so I left orders with the watch-keeper to keep the fucking male chav's off and only let the girls on board. We soon had a mess room full of blonde haired blue eyed beauties having a party and among them were two stunning looking sisters who spoke good English and kept calling me Rod (it was the Rod Stewart thing again) and kept to singing me "Maggie May". I didn't think for one minute they believed I was Rod Stewart but because of the remoteness of the place I was about the nearest they would get to the real thing and I have no doubt that if he could have seen me, he would have called me a lucky sod.

Later the two-sisters invited me back to their house to carry on the party. Well I didn't need inviting twice so along with one of the lads we got two cases of beer and we slipped away quietly. She assured me her parents were out of town for the weekend, "What a result." I thought. "Time to rebel all boarders." After a ten-minute walk we arrived at the house, it was nice, like a luxury wooden chalet. Anyway, we all piled in as you do, there were maybe ten of us in total. Out came the music tapes and on went a cassette tape of Rod Stewart, then the flirting began. "Hang on a minute," I said, taking off my wrangler jacket and I went over to what I thought was a blue marble cupboard, open it and threw the coat in.

"No! no!" shouted one of the girls holding her hands to her face, laughing, looking a little puzzled. "What's wrong?" I said and she walked over, opened the door and pointed and OH SHIT. Then I realised the error of my actions it wasn't a cupboard. I had just thrown my coat into a wood burning stove. Oh well learn from your mistakes and benefit from your achievements I thought and if I get my way I would achieve quite a bit tonight. Let's party!!! Soon the beer started to run out so I decided to go back to the ship with one of the crew for fresh supplies. Sig, one of the sisters, insisted on coming with us, fair enough who wouldn't want to be seen in her company. Anyway, we duly arrived back on the ship and apart from the watch-keeper, everyone had turned in for the night. All except for Bob that was, he was an engine-room motor-man, who made no secret of the fact he liked his beer and he was definitely not on the same planet as he had a skin full and try as we may could not rouse him from his drunken stupor. He was also a bit of an odd bod with women and found it difficult to in-teract with the ladies. But he certainly loved porn his mags, and his cabin was stacked with them. Rumour had it that he only had a little todger, and that he had seen an ad in one of his dirty mags for a penis enlarger, so he paid ten quid, and sent off for one. But it transpired he was not happy when it arrived, it was a magnifying glass. Anyway, cue Mr mischief. We picked him up and took him to his cabin. Now for some fun, we striped him naked, then, I borrowed Sigs lipstick before carefully drawing lip shaped kisses around, (shall we say) the nether region. With that complete we put his piss stained undies on him, back to front, then I asked Sig to plant a smacker on his fore head, that left one final piece of the jigsaw to put into place. Now as any good seaman will tell you just like a boy scout's motto, be prepared, in this case a love glove (condom). In case you were wondering. I don't know if any of you readers remember that disgusting tinned milk you used to get, it looked like white syrup and we called it "sticky licky".

Well the point is, we poured some of this into a condom and left it beside his bunk, I asked Sig to write a love note and sign it Gustave. We left that on his table along with a couple of Swedish cigs, Bob didn't smoke by the way and having got another case of beer it was back to the party, which carried on until it ran out. Once all the freeloading locals had left Sig to lock up and led me into the bedroom. After a lot of steamy passion, Sig got out of bed and soon returned with a couple of cans of beer, in a bucket of ice. Nice touch I thought, but must I desperately needed to drain the snake and so off I went.

When I came back the room was in darkness, so I jumped back in the sack, I could hear mutterings of sweet nothings in Swedish, which I could not understand. She suddenly started speaking English again, "Now I will show you Swedish pleasure," she oozed at me and with that she started running an ice cube all over my body, after getting over the initial shock I must admit it was very erotic. So my theory was simple, anything you can do, I will try and do better, but with a climatic twist that had her squirming in a mind-blowing climax. Details of which I won't go into in case any lady readers get any ideas about finishing the old man off. I have since only used this love ritual twice, with the out-come being the same in both cases but there was an even bigger bonus to come because after the deed was done, the door opened, the light went on and there stood in all her naked glory, was Sig. So who the hell had I just given a good sorting out to? Well to put you all out of your misery it was her sister. I felt like the luckiest man on the earth, that for me was the first and only time, I had ever slept with two women at the same time. I spent the best part of the week-end with the girls but as in all good things in life they surely do come to an end.

Monday saw the ship loaded with a cargo of timber and it was soon time to cast off and sail away. As we were about to leave about a dozen locals turned up, led by the sisters to say goodbye. That I can assure you was one of the saddest days of leaving a port I have ever been in, and by then I had travelled the world. For many years, the warmth of that night kept me company on many a lonely night when on watch as look-out at sea.

By the way, Bob the motorman just never seemed the same man after that and was often observed starring into empty space. I would like to think he was just pining for his Swedish lover Gustav the lumberjack.

The trip back to the U.K was a bit of an anti-climax and we all hoped we would get a return trip, but as with all great plans they usually go tits up. This trip was no exception, before we finished discharging cargo, we were told that we had a cargo waiting for us in Tilbury. Loading grain for Rotterdam and if that was a let-down, worse was to come, the skipper was overdue for leave and his re-placement was on his way. And so Titanic Ted enters my story.

TITANIC TED

Going to sea could be full of adventures but also full of dangers and drama. When the skipper who was going on leave told me who his replacement was the hair on the back of my neck rose, TITANIC TED. I wouldn't reveal his real   name, suffice to say that his first name was Ted. Although I had never sailed with him be-fore, he was a legend in the company and was credited with more ship disasters than of Lloyds of London. He was also said to be a lazy bastard, who did as least amount of work he could get away with. So, the stage was set. Captain Ted duly arrived and after tak-ing command went to his cabin. Now Ted was well in his sixties and by the look of him should have got a shore job years ago after running Noah's ark aground.

However, he was here now and I would be sleeping with one eye open. Once we got to sea one of the crew came to me and told me. My presence was required in Teds cabin. Wonder what the fuck does he want I thought. So, I duly held court with the merchant navy's answer to the Red Baron. As Bosun I was given the usual lecture of how he liked his ship run. "You come highly thought of by the company matey," he went on. "Keep the deck crew in line and everything will be honky dory," he droned on, lecture over. I told him I was off ashore to make a phone call home.

So off I went to the pub (well that was where the nearest phone was). Feeling a bit sorry for myself I ordered a pint, then did an ET and "phoned home" good job. Luck was about to smile on me. In the shape of a very well paid job offer with a Norwegian diving ship company. Working one month away and one month at home. I jumped at the chance and as the next crew change had just been done. I had a month to give my notice in and get a bit of shore leave, sorted. What could possible go wrong, famous last words.

We duly finished discharging our load and made ready for sea. We had only been underway for less than an hour before Titanic Ted started to live up to his reputation. We were sat in the mess room, when the tannoy squawked into life, it was Captain Ted, "Is the Bosun there?" he asked. "Tell him to come to the bridge," I duly went up and looking over the top of his glasses Captain Ted said, "Ah, matey I set a course, keep a sharp look out and call the mate out at half past five, I've got some business to do in my cabin, " and he disappeared without so much as a by your leave. "Yeah, yeah," I thought, 'Business in my arse. More like business with that bottle of whiskey I saw on his desk. So now he had lumbered me with doing half of his watch and half of the mates watch, cheeky old bastard.

And, so it went on until we got to Tilbury. Before we docked the Mate called me to one side and announced, "I've had enough, I've sailed with him before and he is still up to his old tricks. I'm asking to take emergency leave, just don't take any crap off the dodgy old sod."

"No problem," I replied and told him of my new job offer, it wasn't long before we started loading cargo the Mate duly left and his replacement arrived. Captain Ted gave him a coat of looking over as we say at sea, and once the new mate was out of ear shot, Captain Ted turned to me and said "Watch him matey" he looks like a right lazy bastard. And "Oooh, bloody hell," I thought, "talk about the pot calling kettle black." Captain Ted was the last one to make a comparison, there was more work in a sick note than Ted. However, I must admit there was something strange about the new mate, he looked like a troubled man, on the edge. It would be an observation that would turn out to be true sooner than I though. Once we had loaded cargo and battened down the hatches, so to speak. We took the pilot on board, cast off and made our way up the river, seawards.

I went onto the bridge reported that everything was stowed and secure as was the normal. One of the duties of a Captain is too remain on the bridge until the pilot is dropped off. But, as you readers are aware by now Titanic Ted was far from a normal Captain and he was soon up to his normal tricks making the usual apologies, and leaving the bridge. I soon followed suit and went into the mess room on standby for when we dropped the pilot off. After we cleared the river and dropped off the pilot, I decided to call it an early night and lay on top of my pram reading. Within an hour or so there was a shuddering of the ship and the engines stopped.

I was quickly out of my bunk and I put on my work boots. I made my way onto the deck fearing we had hit another ship. The coast was clear of any other ship, then the reality sunk in, the curse of Titanic Ted, had awoken. We had run aground. I rushed up to the bridge to be confronted by a ghostly white faced lookout, who simply pointed a finger at the corner of the bridge. Looking around I saw the mate curled up in a tight ball, blubbering away like a demented seal hunter. "What the fuck is wrong with him?" I yelled.

"I don't know." said the lookout, "he just threw a wobbler, changed course, then sat in the corner banging his head."

"Go and get the skipper up here now." I shouted, and added angrily, "that's if he's fucking sober." I quickly started going over to the chart table and looked for our position. Oh shit we had hit one of the most notorious sand banks in the world. The Goodwin, a graveyard for ships. By now the ship to shore radio was alive with chatter, the coastguard had spotted us on radar and wanted an update. I requested a lifeboat and they dispatched one to our assistance too standby in case of the worst. With that the bridge door opened and in strolled Captain Ted as leisurely as you like and as cool as a cucumber. He looked straight at me he said, "This is a fine old mess you have got us into matey isn't it."

I was fucking livid, "Me! Me!" I shouted back "You useless old bastard," I had lost it now. "You should have been up here and just for the log book, it's that useless piece of shit there who ran us aground." I said pointing at the Mate rolling about the floor like a nut case. And with a face like thunder he just strolled past the mate and stepped over him like he wasn't there and he went onto the wing of the bridge, looked over the side for a couple of minutes before returning, where he looked at me and announced, "Well matey" he said,   "at least we cannot sink."

"Well fucking whoopee." I snapped back, "sink! Sink!" I yelled, "how very fucking reassuring. So what are you going to do about it Captain?" I said sarcastically."

"Do? Do?" he repeated and looked at the chart, "Luckily we are aground on a solid bed of sand, the tide is going out, so there is nothing we can do until it comes in again."

Well I had to agree, because when it comes to experience in running ships aground he must surely be the world's expert.

"Let me know when the lifeboat arrives on station," he said and left the bridge. After what seemed an eternity the lifeboat arrived. Just then Captain Ted reappeared as she came alongside and one of her crew made his way onto the bridge. "Can I be of assistance captain?" he asked Captain Ted, who simply looked at the mate, who was still blubbering and muttering away in the corner of the bridge.

"Yes" he said simply, "you can get that mumbling piece of trash of my ship. We will try and re-float at, high tide."

To say that the tensions where running high amongst the crew would be an understatement and once we had a good luck around to see if we had been holed and were satisfied there were no holes and the ship was watertight all we could do was wait for high tide. Eventually the tide rose enough for us to attempt to re-float the ship and with the aid of the lifeboat and a lot of strain on the engine, we finally freed ourselves.

Happy as we could be that the ship was seaworthy as she could be, we made passage to Rotterdam, with me as a stand in for the mate, who I suspect would never go back to sea again. I had been studying to take my mate's ticket and had the relevant qualifications it was deemed acceptable. Thank god there were no more mishaps and we duly arrived in port to begin discharge. We were due to sail at three pm the next day.

On the morning of sailing and after making all the necessary safety checks Captain Ted informed me," I am going ashore on business matey, I will be back before the pilot comes aboard and while we are on the subject," he carried on, "I didn't like the way you spoke to me yesterday, I am the captain and you should show respect."

Well I wasn't in the mood for another lecture from him and told him in no uncertain terms that to earn respect, you must also show respect. I certainly was not going to be anyone's scapegoat especially his. We left it at that and off he went ashore. I think that was the time I realised that life is a mirror, whilst you can consider it and reflect upon the past you cannot see into the future.

From that day on I never took anything for granted except the fact that the sea can always be unpredictable and unforgiving. I also concluded that he was something of a sad and lonely man, who it seemed at times to be a tormented soul, especially when I saw him staring into space. What was going on his mind was anyone's guess and I too came to the belief that people only think when they have nothing to say. Well enough of the philosophy for now, when we get back to London, I was packing my kit bag and off.

At about half past two the pilot arrived, along with Captain Ted who was carrying a rather large parcel. It might have been a new mattress, as he must have worn his own out the amount of time he spent on it, but it was too small. Anyhow we duly cast off and headed out to sea. After dropping the pilot off we set course for the Thames, duty watches were set and to my surprise, Captain Ted told me he would take the first watch and I could go and get my head down.

When I crawled into my bunk I realised I had been up for nearly thirty hours straight and I didn't need no rocking, I was soon in the land of nod.

Sometime later I awoke with a start looking at my watch, I had been throwing Z's off for nearly eight hours and as I got out of my pram, there was a knock on the door. It was the watch-keeper, "Oh your already up," he said handing me a mug of tea for which I was grateful. I got washed and dressed then went to relieve Captain Titanic Ted on the bridge only to be greeted with, "Back with us are you matey," he seemed to say sarcastically with the nearest thing to a smile he could muster.

Shock number two swiftly followed, turning to the watch-keeper, he told him to go and have half an hour break. When he had gone, Captain Ted said he wanted to set aside our differences then proceeded to tell me a rather sad story about his life. His life, it had turned out that at one time he was a highly regarded and respected Captain and a pillar of his local community until (sadly as was sometimes the case for seamen) his wife had jumped ship while he was away on a trip, and done a bunk, with a landscape gardener. Presumably he was trimming her bush, anyway when he got home a few months later she had sold the house, its contents and wiped out his bank balance, never to be seen again.

Well somehow he managed to get back on his feet again, although a broken and sad man he bought himself a modest little house and tried to get on with his life, like trying to sink ships I thought, but I kept quiet. This is where the old saying of, 'there's no fool like an old fool,' as he then went on to explain, that he had met a cheap freeloading prostitute, who bizarrely he had let move into his house.

Now, as I said at the beginning of this book. I call it as I see it, and on this occasion, tact and diplomacy seemed to desert me. "Shit," I said, "You can't carry on like this Captain. For all you know, she could be using your house as a bloody knocking shop. And one day the same thing might happen to you again. You don't want to finish your days at sea, sad and skint. And to be blunt, if you do, one day you might be found dead in your bunk and I for one would not like to see that happen."

He posed for a moment, before saying, "You know what young man," and he looked deep at me, "you are right. Its time I stopped feeling sorry for myself. When I get home, I'm going to get rid of her, and keep what little money I have left."

Looking at him I somehow doubted he would do what he said, "Go and get your head down Captain," I advised him. "I will give you a call before we pick up the Thames pilot." And with that, without a word he left the bridge.

The trip back was uneventful and before we knew it we were at the pilot station and having safely navigated past the Goodwin Sands, we picked up the pilot and were soon heading up the river. I told the bridge lookout to go and get Captain up.

After about five minutes the look-out was back on bridge looking as white as a sheet, "What's wrong with you?" I asked. He was shaking like a plate of jelly in a gale of wind. "Well? Spit it out?" I asked again, Is he out of his scratching pit yet?"

"I don't know." was the nervous reply, "I think he's croaked."

"Fuck!." I said automatically, "what the hell are you on about? I demanded to know.

"Well," he carried on, "I knocked on his cabin and went in. The lights are not working, but I can see him in the dark gloom sat his desk rigid and not moving. He wouldn't answer me."

A cold shiver ran down my back, this cannot be real, it was only yesterday that I jokingly said if he didn't buck up they would find him dead. I should not have said it.

By now the Pilot steering he ship in was looking at me. "Are you going to check?" the pilot asked?

"Oh, shit. I suppose someone must, not that I want to."

I left the bridge and posed outside his cabin door. Plucking up courage to go in I had visions of him sat there looking like Captain Ahab on the back of Moby Dick, with one arm flapping as if to beckon me over. Get a grip man and take possession of yourself, I heard myself saying.

I knocked on his door slowly opened it, and went inside. As my eyes got accustomed to the gloom I could clearly see him sat at his desk. "Captain? Captain?" I whispered, "the pilots on board." No answer only silence. I asked again, "Captain are you all right?" and with that his bedroom door creaked open and there stood the Captain, "Arrgh!" I shouted in panic, "your stupid old bastard. We thought you had snuffed it, you nearly gave me a heart attack," I came over all unnecessary,

As I looked around at his desk and in the gloom of his bedroom light all was revealed, the body in the chair was a pumpy up doll, the old fool must have bought it ashore, somehow blew it up, then got pissed and turned in. "I'm on my way," he said with panic in his voice, "and not a word to anyone, about this matey," he warned.

I had resigned myself that he had snuffed it, I returned to the bridge and informed the pilot that it was a simple mistake and he was coming up. He duly appeared looking a bit sheepish and after introducing himself to the pilot, he pretended to busy himself with the charts after a short while the pilot piped up. "Would anyone like a sweet?" and he held out a bag of sweets.

Well I just could not resist a golden opportunity to have a dig at Ted, "Oh don't mind if I do," I replied, "what kind are they Dolly mixtures?"

"Oh I like Dolly mixtures," piped up the lookout.

"No said the pilot they are humbugs."

"Bah Humbug," I thought. However, I was not about to let Titanic Ted off the hook that easily. "I haven't seen Dolly mixtures for a long time." I carried on.

By this time Captain was getting a little uncomfortable, so I changed the subject, much to his relief, but I haven't finished with him yet. "I was doing a crossword yesterday," I said, "and there was just one answer I couldn't get."

"What was it?" asked the pilot, "I like crosswords."

"Well," I answered, "the clue was a hit single for Cliff Richard, six and four letters."

After a pause, the thick sod of a look-out said, "I think I know this one, is it Summer Holiday."

"No, your clueless clown," I laughed, again a short pause. "Then eureka declared the pilot, "Got it, its Living Doll.

"Oh, yeah," I replied, "Well done."

The pilot carried on, "It came to me after you mentioned dolly mixtures."

Piping up in the background the watch keeper, went to say, "Personally I don't like Cliff Richard. I prefer country and western, so who is your favourite, I enquired.

And without cracking his face, the watch keeper innocently said, "Why Dolly Parton of course."

Well that was it poor old Captain Ted could take no more, innuendos, he flared up, "Can't you lot talk about fucking something other than bloody dolls." and stormed off into the chartroom, the poor old pilot looked absolutely stunned and whispered to me. "What's wrong with him?"

"Just ignore the grouchy old git." I replied, "word has it that his parents wanted a girl, and instead of normal boy's toy's at xmas they bought him a dolls pram."

"Oh, poor sod," answered the pilot laughing, "no wonder he's pissed off."

We carried on up river to tilbury, as soon as we tied up and put the gangway out, my relief turned up leaving me with just the formalities of getting changed and signing off. But not before Captain Ted tried to get me to change my mind, not a bloody chance I was off.

Looking back on this story I wonder if the poor old sod took my advice and dumped the two- legged dog out of his life. I doubt it.

God bless you Captain Ted where ever you are. I never heard about, or bumped in Captain Titanic Ted ever again. But I'm sure wherever he was he took his doll.

UNDER MY SPELL

Life goes on as they say and having finally said goodbye to Titanic Ted and leaving him to his nautical adventures or should that be disasters, I concentrated on my new job.

But first I had some catching up to do at home, I did the usual routine of going to the pub's, night clubs and reminding some of the local girls what they missed and I have woken up on more than one occasion, next to a red-hot bit of totty. And have to sadly admit woken up next to some dogs as well and wondered what the hell I had to drink the night before and quietly got dressed and tip toed out the bedroom and got a taxi home. Life's strange thing and like most randy teenagers I had my moments.

So now back to business the day duly arrived, when once again I said my goodbyes to family and loved ones and set of for Aberdeen on the next leg of my adventures. When I got there, I was pleasantly surprised at the ship compared to the last one. It was like a luxury liner, with all the bells and whistles. I knew I had done the thing, as any seaman will tell you, you get a certain feeling when joining a new ship and I had a good feeling about this one. Once I had reported to Captain I found my cabin and met the rest of the crew. They all seemed a good bunch and it did help that three of them were from Hull and I soon settled in. We were in dock two days when we were told we had landed a lucrative six-month contract servicing the gas platforms off Great Yarmouth. So off we jolly well go then. It was a time of busy activity and we soon got into a well drilled rhythm. Once we finished one inspection, it was on to another.

We would return to port for a couple of days, before starting again. Whilst there were the usual number of pubs in Yarmouth. Mostly as expected busy in the summer with holiday makers and as dead as tomb in Winter. There was also a seaman's mission down the docks. By that I mean it was a pre-fab building and not a bad size. After a while we got quite friendly with the couple who ran it and had a good banter going with them. We were in port for the weekend and the skipper decided to split the crew into two watches. I drew lucky which meant I got Saturday afternoon and Saturday night off, making me a very happy chappie. So, once the watches were set I and two of my shipmates decided that as the Sun was over the yard-arm as they say, it was time to go ashore. We duly arrived at the seaman's mission when I decided to have a bit of fun with the landlord. We went up to the bar and tapped on it, strutting over John the landlord looked at us and said, "And what do you reprobates want?"

Putting on my poshest accent, I proffered, "Greetings bar keeper, may we per chance purchase have three strawberry daiquiris, with a twist of lime if you please."

Raising one eye brow and looking like silent movie actor Ben Turpin out of a Laurel and Hardy films he merely replied, "You can piss off and have your usual lagers."

"Oh, come, come my good man," I carried on, "is that anyway to speak to your paying clientele?"

"Now do you want three beers or what?" he replied.

"OK," one of the lads joined in, "but, make sure you pull them from the tap behind the bar and not the one in the gent's bog and we want them with a head on. The last lot you as gave us were as flat as a witches' tits, "

The Landlord just laughed and pulled the pints, "So is your mob coming in tonight to see the show he enquired?"

 We carried on baiting him, "And what show might that be then John, you trying to pull a decent pint, "I ragged him but he was not biting.

"You know what I mean," he carried on, "The hypnotist, he is getting rave reviews he is. He will be a big star one day." And how right he was.

Well we had another pint, then up town, to sample a few more pints. We went into one of the back street, which would have made miss Father Sham's cottage look sterile.

Well this time one of the lads tried winding up another landlord putting on a few heirs and graces. "Greetings landlord, per chance may I purchase three pints of your finest and world renowned cask ales." Well I knew it was a mistake and tried to persuade my shipmate that it wouldn't be a wise thing to do, but against my best advice he was having none of it. The alarm bells should have rung, especially as the landlord had a face like a vandalised back street junk shop. Scowling and with the humour of an undertaker, he snapped back, "Are you taking the fucking piss?"

To which my shipmate replied cheekily, "Why haven't you got any beer?"

And that was it the Landlord pulled out a baseball bat from under the bar. Quicker than a horny prossi could get a horny sailors todger out, we took the less than subtle hint that this hovel was not worthy of such genteel clientele such as ourselves and bolted before he took a swing at us with base ball bat. To the sound of, "And don't fucking come back, you cheeky bastards I run a re-spectable pub."

Well we knew that was a lie because looking at the filthy bastard, it was hard to imagine him running a descent bath. Well we spent the rest of the afternoon cruising from pub to pub and in our last port of call, before heading back to the mission, we went for one last pint in a popular tourist pub.

Now I'm sure you readers are more than aware that most pubs seem to have a resistant free loader on the lookout for a free drink, this pub was no exception. We sat down and I felt a hand on my shoulder and I turned to face the owner of the filthy digits stroking my shoulder like a long friend. And there stood a drink induced old bag with this big lost smile on her face. And by the smell of her, I deduced she had run out of cheap perfume and resorted to a quick dab of toilet duck behind each ear and staring at me through blood shot eyes, she said, "You don't half look like Rod Stewart. I think he is the sexiest man alive." And adding with a wistful, "You can have my body anytime," then pouted her lips in my direction. Unfortunately, she seemed to have missed her gob, with the lipstick, and had a red moustache instead.

"Listen," I said in a diplomatic voice, "I'm a seaman, not an undertaker and if you're after getting a free drink. You have got more chance of sticking a wet noodle up a Tigers arse." I must have offended her in some way because she snapped back, with breath that would have made a bunged-up toilet smell fresh. "I've heard about sailors," she carried on in an acidic voice, "dirty underpants and no fucking money." That reminded me I must do my laundry when I get back to the ship.

Shock, horror, our good name and reputation had been besmirched, one of the lads was quick to defend our honour, taking the piss he said, "listen you wizened old hag I will have you know, we do have money and you aren't getting any."

Thankfully the old crow got the message, and spying what to her looked like an easier target, she pissed off, but not before knocking a table of drinks over and protesting at us, "Who the fuck you pushing, I'm a lady." And she staggered out the door looking for some other mugs.

The fun was over and time was ticking, so we drank up and set sail back to the mission for what would turn out to be a very memorable night.

We duly arrived, at the mission, where two more members of our crew had set up camp and saved us seat's. We got our tonsil varnish and joined them. Well it was a long walk from the town and even camels need a drink and we were chucking them down like there was tomorrow. By this time the place was nearly full.

As we were chewing the rug, there was a "chink, chink" of a glass to get the patron's attention. "Ladies and gentlemen," she started to announce the act coming on, "oh and you lot of hairy arsed sailors over there," and she got a big laugh. "As you know tonight we have a special treat for you, this man is destined to be a big star of the future, please welcome "Mr Paul McKenna." A cheer and big round of applause went up.

There were five chairs, lined up in front of the bar. "Right your salty sea-dogs," announced Paul McKenna, "I want five mugs. Sorry volunteers."

It can never be said that seamen where backward when it came to coming forward and several hands shot up. McKenna milled around the tables and picked five, mugs, sorry victims. Once sat down he put them in a trance, he then touched two of them on the shoulder and informed them their services were not wanted, in other words they were just taking the piss and he knew it. They didn't argue, it must have been true, the three remaining sleeping beauties seemed to be well out of it. Going to the first one he put a hand on his shoulder and said, "When you hear this song (Old McDonald) you will be a chicken looking for food." Turning to number two, he again put his hand on his shoulder saying. "When you hear this song (sound of music) you will see that everyone in here are naked and you will strip off your clothes," Then turning his attention to number three. He went on and you my friend, "When you hear this song (I'm bad). You will become the greatest ballerina in the world, you will dance between the tables, without touching any of them."

Now before I carry on let me just say that the third bloke looked like a bigger version of Oliver Hardy and just as clumsy, so this was going to be interesting to say the least. Anyhow he woke them out of their trance and they duly returned to their seats, or in the case of the fat bloke, two seats. It wasn't long before the fun started, first The Sound of Music. This bloke just stared at everyone in total bewilderment before getting up and starting to strip off, much to everyone's amusement and as soon as he got to his skidies the music stopped.

Now to be fair everyone played along with it and just looked at him like he was an escapee from the local nut farm. I have never seen anyone look so embarrassed, he kept apologising to everyone and didn't have a bloody clue what was going on. Credit where its due, he put his clothes on quicker than he took them off, as he was still wondering what had happened. The song Old McDonald had a farm came on and this other idiot was up and strutting his stuff. He wandered off outside and when the music stopped he came back in looking even more confused than the stripper. It was now time for what was surely the highlight of the evening, cue music, I'm bad. I'm bad Michael Jackson, I think everyone was stunned at the way the Oliver Hardy lookalike, jumped up and I kid you not this bloke moved with the grace of a world class ballet dancer and as predicated, he waltzed and glided around the tables, without touching one of them. Well after prancing about for a few minutes, he was beginning to sweat like a busy whore on a hot summer night and again the music stopped and some sort of normality returned.

I'm sure most people have seen this sort of act on television and thought it's a set up, but believe me having witnessed this show, I can say without question, there was no way this was rigged, however whilst there was a pause in proceedings and it was my round I darted for the gents to stroke the swans neck. So to speak as I was going through the motions the door opened and the fat bloke appeared taking the mickey. I jokingly enquired, "You all right mate you look a bit flushed," as I vaguely knew him he replied, "I think so. I can only remember hearing a song and then I came over all unnecessarily."

"That's bad," I carried on taking the piss, and with that I knew what was coming so I quickly darted into trap one and shut the door quick. Just in time as Tinkerbelle launched into full swing the music stopped nearly as quick as it had started. So, I carefully opened the door, only to see the fat guy covered in piss and holding his head, again wondering what the hell was happening. It was time for a spot of diplomacy I thought. "Bloody hell is it raining outside." I asked. Now the poor sod was in a bit of a state so I decided not to take the piss any further because judging by the state of him, he didn't have any left in him. Fortunately, a thirty-minute recess was called for a bit of badgering and banter to take place. Despite all the piss taking excuse the pun not one of the three guinea pigs, would not believe a word of it when others described what McKenna had made them do.

ROUND TWO

The three amigos where duly summoned and put under the spell again, touching this bloke on the shoulder he told him that when he heard the Tom Jones song, It's not unusual, he would be a preacher from the deep south of America. Then touching the bloke who had previously striped on the shoulder, he told him when he heard the same song, he would have an itchy arse and the only way to stop it would be to drag it across the floor, like a dog. Touching poor old fat bloke on the shoulder, he again said when you hear the same music, you will become Patrick Swazy and start dirty dancing. Snapping them out of it, they returned to their seats, he waited for them to have a good glug of their beer. Before the fun started and Tom Jones, started warbling, and as quick as a flash the fat bloke was up grating around like a chimp with piles, followed by butch the dog, who couldn't wait to stop the itching and promptly started dragging his arse around the floor with his tongue hanging out, he was clearly enjoying the relief. Enter the fray, the right Reverend Mole Turd spiting fire and brimstone. "Resist my children, resist the evil temptations of Satan, smite him down, banish this evil from the light. Sooo say, eth the lord, oh, yah, halleluiah." And it was amazing he did actually sound like one of them Southern state gospel preacher's and while he was rambling on Butch the dog was happily trying to lick his arse, with fat man having somehow to get behind the bar, started doing pelvic thrusts up the leg of the horrified barmaid. Having spotted this outrageous behaviour. The right Reverend Mole Turd, launched into sermon, "Harlot!" he shouted, "desist from your lewd behaviour, resist the temptation of naked flesh. Soo sayeth the lord, oooh! Yeah! Halleluiah." And fat bloke's reward rubbing his willy up the barmaid's leg was a smack in the kisser. Not that it bothered him and he merely started getting raunchy with a chair. Having given up on trying to lick his own arse, Butch the dog carried on dragging his itchy arse across the floor. The whole place was in uproar with laughter and the music stopped once again and it seemed the only people who didn't have a clue what was going on, was the three stooges. But as the saying goes all good things must come to end and we piled out the mission pissed to the gunnels and staggered to the quay side. And I must admit this was one of the best nights I have ever had. I can't remember what happened after that. But I had one hell of hang over the next morning.

BILLY BUNTER

Whilst some people may read this and think that all seamen did was go ashore get drunk and cause mayhem. It's not true believe me. When we were at sea we worked hard and risked life and limb daily. I know myself by having many injuries, but enough of the seriousness, now let's get back to the fun times.

After yet another two weeks of non- stop work in the gas fields, we returned to Yarmouth, when the Captain announced that in the interest of good will, the company, along with others would be having an open day for the public. To give them an insight to what we did and, "Shit that's my plans gone out of the port-hole," I thought. The big event was to be held on the Sunday and all shore was cancelled. Well, after unloading all the equipment from our latest adventure, it was time to prepare for the main event. The gods must have been smiling on us, because the weather was excellent, warm and sunny. Soon the quayside was thronging with holiday-makers and locals alike, everything was going swimmingly as they say. The cook had laid on plenty of nibbles and tit-bits (don't get smutty) I'm referring to savouries. Anyhow everything was going smoothly, when the unexpected happened. What looked like the SLOBS family out of the Harry Enfield show turned up looking like they had gotten their new outfits from a discarded charity shop bag of clothes. Mr slob was a skinny weasel faced chav, with a filthy track suit bottoms, Mrs slob was even worse, dressed like someone from a budget Oxfam appeal advert. She had more stubble on her chin than Mr slob. Now bringing up the rear was an overweight Eddie Munster lookalike, with a serious attitude problem

I was showing a nice couple around the deck, when Eddie Munster pushed his way in, "Oi mister," he said with a gormless grin on his ugly mush, time for a wind up and the little chav was in for a treat. "Yes young man?" I asked, "what can I do for you?" Wiping his snotty sniffer on the back of his already filthy rag of a coat, "Got any hotdogs, my mam said it was free nosh."

I'll see what I can do for you." I answered trying to be polite and professional. "When I've finished talking to these nice people."

"I'm hungry now," he ranted on.

"OK Eddie," I smarted back, "bea good little boy and be patient and I will go and see."

"My name isn't Eddie," he whined, "its Clint."

I coughed and bit my tongue. "Right you little (I had to choose the next word very carefully) right Clint," I said through my gritted teeth, "Wait there." And I went and found the cook and told him the little fat chav wanted a hot dog. I didn't need to point him out, "Oh fucking Eddie Munster you mean, that little fat bastards, they been eating anything that's not nailed down and Wayne and Wauneta slob, have been filling their pockets right, I'll give the prick a hot dog, come with me to the galley." As it happened we had plenty spare. So, we got to work on a seaside special, he cut a hot dog right down the middle, then soaked it in Tabasco sauce, after putting it back together and smothered it in onions. "Nice one Kevin," I smiled. "Let me do the honours. The little bastard won't ask for another one."

"Oh I have to see this," said Kev and off we went in search of our victim, which wasn't hard as he was loitering around the table we had set up on deck. As soon as he spotted us, he was like a fly round shit, "Where's my hotdog mister?"

"Here you go Eddie," I said handing it over to him.

"I've told you my name not Eddie its Clint"

"Of course it is," I replied sarcastically, "and a right little (pause), Clint you are too". I said, "Enjoy your hot dog." Well he slotted it down quicker than an M.P. filling in their expenses. We both stood back and waited for mount Edna to erupt but, nothing happened. We couldn't believe it this kid must have had a stomach like a mountain I goat. "Got anymore mister?"

Kev retaliated, "More, you want more boy?"

"Yeah and not so many onions, my mam said they give you the shits." Looking at the state of her, who would notice anyway. Before we could go and reload with a real arse burner of a hotdog something strange happened through the grime Eddie's face lit up like an agitated squid on heat, flashing all manner of colours, he spun around and unleashed a broad side of foul smelling spluttering bile straight out of his mouth. Unfortunately, the poor woman behind him copped the lot right down her neck and her best Sunday-dress. The world seemed to stop, it was like slow motion, she slowly turned around, but before she could utter a single word, the husband was on the scene.

"You filthy, disgusting little bastard," he screamed into his face, we could see what was coming next, as he griped Eddie by the scruff of his filthy shirt collar, and before he could experience what would probably have been the first bath of his life. We reluctantly stepped in, "OK mate we will deal with it, your wife can clean herself up in my cabin while we sort this out. And Kev ushered them away and pleading his innocence and the ungrateful little bastard tried pinning the blame on us.

After all the trouble we went too that's bloody gratitude for you.

"They poisoned me, Eddie Munster protested but plea that fell on deaf ears I hasten to add. And with that Mr and Mrs slob appeared, grabbed him by the scruff of his neck, Mrs slob had the audacity to say. "What have I told you about showing me up in public, wait until I get you home, you will feel the back of my hand. The filthy cow then glared at me, "This is your fault for giving him all that food, he doesn't eat a lot at home."

"Madam," I said very politely, "that kid of yours would embarrass a glutton." Not wishing to cause a diplomatic incident, I pointed out the errors of her ways. "Firstly, Mrs in the interest of public hygiene, may I suggest, when taking him out for walkies, it might be sensible to fit him with a muzzle and by judging by what I've seen of you lot today. The reason he doesn't eat a lot at home is properly because the greedy little fat bastard hasn't got any room left." Her response was hardly unexpected, "You can fuck off. I've got a good mind to report you to the public health." Looking her up and down, I could see she was clearly no stranger to that organisation and as they started their decent down the gangway, a voice in the crowd shouted, "Get a bath and a shave chav."

Well the families name had been called into question and farther Slop was not going to let that insult go by without a response and a bit of a one way slanging match took place as they went down the gang plank. "I've had a bath and a shave." he shouted back and another voice shouted, "We aren't talking to you, we were talking to your wife." Well that comment was met with a big round of applause and laughter.

The rest of the day went off without incident, a good time was had by all and by six o' clock the ship was empty so we decided to head for the seaman's mission. Well it would have been rude not to. As soon as we entered John the manager beat us to the draw, "We haven't got any daiquiris with a twist of lemon left," he snapped before we could take the piss. Thinking he had got one over us, the poor misguided fool was in for a shock, "In that case bar-keeper my good man, we will settle for three rum-be-bah with just a hint of mint," His right eyebrow raised as was his usual re-sponse, "That's three lager's then."

We had many memorable times whilst working out of great Yar-mouth, and gained a good reputation whilst there, that was until we spoiled it. Xmas was soon upon us, and our contract was end-ing. About four days before Christmas we decided to festoon the ship with Chrsitmas lights. We were to stay in port until after the big day, but as usual events at sea have a bad habit of going tits up, and this was no exception. We were in the mission when one of the crew came in and told us we had to sail, as one of the rigs needed some urgent spares. Bloody Hell was our first comment, but that was our Job, and it had to be done. So we all trooped off back to the ship, and waited for this so-called emergency cargo. It was about one in the morning when it arrived, and we were not amused. It was a metal box about the size of a small fridge. Among its contents believe it or not, was xmas decorations but there were also some spare parts, probably added to justify sending us out to sea in the bad weather. Well we were determined to leave a legacy of our six-month contract in Yarmouth. So as we prepared to cast off the Skipper put all the lights on, and played "I'm dreaming of a white Christmas over the loud speakers as we slowly edged our way up river towards seawards and all the house lights started to come on ashore. And next the harbour master was going ballistic on the V.H.F. radio, we certainly woke the locals up, so much so that even a police car followed us up the quayside with his blue lights flashing. But we were out of reach of the coppers. Happy Days.

There was a sting in the tail however, when we got to the rig the weather was, shall we say a little bit lumpy, I was on deck, and when the crane driver lowered his hook, I just managed to connect it when a rogue wave hit us and the container shot up into the air, and as I dived out of the way I slipped, and did the splits, ouch! the pain was unbelievable. Even worse than that of an M.P being told he can't claim for a packet of biscuits on expenses.

Well as we were only two hours from port and we headed back to port. I was in so much pain that I could not even help to moor up the ship. The next day I was sent to the quacks who confirmed that I had a rupture and would have to go home.

When I got back to the ship I was surprised that we had got away with our antics from the night before in Yarmouth with just a slapped wrist. Fortunately, most people saw the funny side of it including the coppers. I was soon packed, and with a heavy heart and I said good bye to my good friends, and ship mates and headed back to Hull. When I finally got home I went to see my doctor, and was told it could take up to six months to get the operation done, sod that. I asked him to get in touch with St. Thomas Hospital in London because there was a ward there called Dreadnaught which was for seamen and their families paid for by ship owners. So within three weeks I was booked in. I spent five days in hospital before being discharged and sent home. I was feeling as rough as a hedgehog's arse when I got back and spent seven weeks recovering before re-joining my ship. So, the time has come for me to say anchors aweigh as I set sail to see what new adventures awaited me, and what mayhem and mischief I could cause. But before I go I will leave you with this advice.

Words of Wisdom

Thinking? It's all in your mind.

It's better to be nice than nasty.

Trust in those who trust in you

Then there can be no distrust.

If life was all plain sailing

There would be nothing to smooth over.

When someone put's you down

Simple, stand up.

You can look into a mirror and reflect on the past

But you cannot see into the future. So, enjoy each day.

Learn from your mistakes

Benefit from your achievements. Only losers fail.

When someone tells, you they don't have the time

Tell them to get a watch.

The meaning of life is a question.

Questions, require knowledge.

Knowledge, gives you answers?

Equals The meaning of life.

THE END...For now.